To Find

the

Biggest

Tree

Author Wendell Flint.

To Find the Biggest Tree

By Wendell D. Flint
Photography by Mike Law

SEQUOIA NATURAL HISTORY ASSOCIATION

To Find the Biggest Tree
© 2002 Sequoia Natural History Association
First Edition
First Printing December 2002
Printed on recycled paper in Hong Kong through Global Interprint, Inc.

Written by Wendell D. Flint
Photos by Mike Law, except as noted
Book design and production by Jamison Design/Jamison Spittler
Editing and project coordination by Mark Tilchen
Map of California by Eureka Cartography, Berkeley, California
Map sources for redwood and sequoia locations derived from California Department of
Forestry and Fire Protection, and U.S. Forest Service

Library of Congress Cataloging-in-Publication Data

Flint, Wendell D.
　　To find the biggest tree / Wendell D. Flint. — 1st ed.
　　　p. cm.
　　Includes bibliographical references (p.　).
　　ISBN 1-878441-09-4
　　　1. Giant sequoia—California.　2. Giant sequoia—Oregon.
　　3. Coast redwood—California.　4. Coast redwood—Oregon.
　　I. Title.
　　SD397.G52F55 2002
　　634.9'758'09794—dc21

2002007742

Published by
The Sequoia Natural History Association
HCR 89 Box 10
Three Rivers, CA 93271
(559) 565-3759
http://www.sequoiahistory.org

Sequoia Natural
History Association

The non-profit Sequoia Natural History Association works in partnership with the National Park Service to provide educational publications and programs for Sequoia and Kings Canyon National Parks and Devils Postpile National Monument. All income of the Association is devoted to national park scientific and educational endeavors. We offer a variety of educational programs to the public. To participate or to learn more, refer to our address or website above.

Cover photo: Homer's Nose with inset of Mike Law (left) and Wendell Flint by Mike Law.

Back photo: General Sherman Tree by Dick Burns.

Sequoia rings photo: Steve Bumgardner.

Table of Contents

GENERAL SHERMAN

FOREWORD

On May 2, 2002, as this book was in the final design stage, author Wendell Flint passed away. The Big Tree hunter had spent thousands of hours and the last four years of his life dedicated to completing the research required to produce this book. The sequoia trees lost a friend and we will miss his gentle spirit, enthusiasm, and sense of humor.

Flint was a man consumed with a passion for Big Trees. He spent more time measuring these mighty trees than any other person and never lost sight of the fact that what was truly important was to admire and protect them. A retired mathematics teacher from the small city of Coalinga on the western edge of California's Great Central Valley, he spent over fifty years searching for and measuring giant sequoias. In this new edition of *To Find the Biggest Tree*, Flint leads us down many a forest trail, with a "big one," perhaps a new champion, just around the bend.

Mike Law shares the author's enthusiasm for the giant sequoias. Mike photographed hundreds of specimens during the thirty years he assisted Wendell in the search for the largest trees on the earth. Mike and his wife Belinda make their home in the San Gabriel Valley town of Temple City, California. He is a graphic artist creating signs for schools.

To Find the Biggest Tree is far more than a reference manual of statistics and charts. This is a story of rumors, legends, and dreams. It is the story of two men and their lifelong quest to seek out and record, in all their majesty, contenders for the title of the biggest tree in the world. Once readers start following the Big Tree hunters on their journey, they may soon find themselves consumed with the same desire – to ask the question, is that the biggest tree?

Mark Tilchen

EXECUTIVE DIRECTOR OF THE SEQUOIA NATURAL HISTORY ASSOCIATION
SEQUOIA NATIONAL PARK, CALIFORNIA
MAY 2002

General Sherman Tree.
Photograph by Steve Bumgardner.

PREFACE

Tree growth and natural damage will result in changes to the size of the trees discussed in this book. Advances in instrument technology and dating methods may also lead to new information on tree size and age. Since roads and trails may change, we recommend obtaining the latest maps. Obtain permission before venturing onto private land or into areas with signs forbidding trespass. There are instances, such as the Lincolns of Grant Grove and Giant Forest, of more than one tree with the same name. When exploring remote groves, remember, it is up to us to protect the giant sequoias.

On April 15, 2000, as this book was nearing completion, President Clinton established the Giant Sequoia National Monument to protect 327,769 acres of land already a part of the Sequoia National Forest. The purpose of the monument, administered by the Forest Service, is to preserve giant sequoias and the ecosystems upon which they depend. The sequoia groves previously located in Sequoia National Forest now lie within the monument. In this book, I still refer to "Sequoia National Forest" when discussing my work, which occurred before the monument was created. When referring to a grove or tree location I usually use "Giant Sequoia National Monument." The monument is located on National Forest land. Hopefully this will not confuse too many.

The opinions and interpretations presented in this book are solely those of the author and in no way represent those of the National Park Service or any other organization.

INTRODUCTION

This book is about the hunt for the biggest trees in the world. It describes trees that have been recognized for their great size. I took up the quest to find the biggest tree in 1947 and I am still hunting.

To Find the Biggest Tree is not about every sequoia that has been given a name, of which there are many. It is not about groves that lack really big ones nor a text on biology. It is about individual trees that have grown to great size and how to find them. The very reason these trees have been preserved in national parks, national forests, and California State lands *is* that they are the most magnificent and largest living trees on the earth. This book tells about trees that had roads built through them, fallen giants, and tales of reputed giants that shrank a bit when measured. It tells about people who looked for giants and about rumors of the monster tree that is now lost in the forests of the Sierra Nevada and my effort to find it. The theme is bigness. I do deviate from time to time to prattle about some unusual trees.

How To Use This Book

The original data were in the English system. Metric measurements are included in charts and where appropriate. Maps show the location of trees of unusual size or interest. There is always more to see than is indicated on the maps. Abbreviations are used to indicate specific maps. For example, (#1 RM) refers to #1 on the Redwood Mountain Grove map. If a tree has no recognized name, it is given as 'Unnamed' and called by a descriptive abbreviation. For example, 'Npersh' refers to a tree near Pershing. A suggested, unofficial name may also be given. References are provided when appropriate.

Acknowledgments

My sincere appreciation to Mike Law, who took most of the pictures in the book and did the hard work – such as tape stretching. I wish to acknowledge those who provided valuable assistance gathering information. Bob Rogers aided my research on Sequoia National Forest. Dwight Willard recognized the great Ishi Giant and was a fountain of knowledge on the history and status of the sequoia groves. David Dulitz, Forest Manager of the Mountain Home State Forest, helped with maps and data on the Adam Tree. John Palmer and Dick Burns encouraged me to write the first edition of this book. Jerry Latham drove me hither and yon and helped me measure. Bob Walker re-located the Muir Snag and chased down the Homer's Nose Phantom Tree. Ron Hildebrant kept me in touch with what was going on among the coast redwoods and provided redwood tree photos. Robert Van Pelt and Michael Taylor introduced me to finding the tall and big coast redwoods and furnished valuable advice and data. Bill Croft introduced me to the really big coast redwoods. Rudolf W. Becking and Frank Clark furnished me with data on coast redwoods. John Hawksworth furnished valuable information on the Nelder Grove. Stan Hutchinson researched the history of the northernmost groves and worked closely with John Hawksworth. Forest Clingan gave me a source for a rumor and kept me challenged on the order of giant sequoia size. Robert Bergen spotted the rare weeping giant sequoia and often hiked along on my expeditions. Mr. and Mrs. Jake Goodman provided invaluable help tracking down history and places in the Mountain Home area. Dennis Coggins and Brian Hale are co-owners with Jerry Latham and me of our cabin, called *Blithering Heights*, where we do a lot of lip flapping. They hiked with me from time to time. Frederick Myer shared his great knowledge of the Calaveras Groves and more. Mark Tilchen got me to write this new edition and assisted with editing and updating data. Rod Fitch worried about my grammar in the first book and helped with several measurements. Paul Wheeler knew a lot about redwoods with roads through them and Ed Carley tried to use my directions to find things.

Numerous people contributed to the successful completion of this book. Jamison Spittler of Jamison Design provided design and directed production. Marilyn Norton, Barbara Squires, and Alice Daniel spent considerable time editing and proofreading. Mark Tilchen directed the project. Nate Stephenson, Bill Tweed, Tom Henry, and Mike Law provided manuscript review and expert guidance. Margie Andreco, Dayna Bose, Heidi Crouch, Mitra Ganley, Megan E. Hansen, Brooke Koenigsaecker, Bob Meadows, Candy B. Harrington, Georgia Dempsey, and Elissa Wurf assisted with proofreading.

All photographs were taken by Mike Law except where noted. Dayna Bose provided the map concept based on the author's drawings.

Big Tree in Giant Forest.
Photograph by Mark Tilchen.

Early pioneers measure giant sequoia. Photograph from NPS collection, Sequoia National Park.

Chapter 1:

HISTORY AND STUFF

In Search of the Largest Tree

This chapter will get us started on our quest of really big giant sequoias. I will start with a little history, followed by a mercifully short personal account.

Native Americans were the first people to see giant sequoias. They may have regarded them as sacred trees, or as a convenient hunting ground, or just ignored them. Not much is recorded about their interaction with the sequoias, except it has been noted that they burned some areas to increase foliage growth for the deer to eat.

The first pioneer to see them was a member of the Joseph Walker party of 1833.[1] There are traces of earlier claims, all unsubstantiated. Zeno Leonard, from the Walker Party, said in his diary that these trees were 16 to 18 fathoms or 35 meters around – a figure in keeping with the truth-stretching abilities of our California pioneers.[2] I'll concede these trees must have seemed huge to them. Leonard's find was probably in the Merced or Tuolumne groves, now part of Yosemite National Park.[3]

In the spring of 1852, Augustus Dowd chased a grizzly bear into the North Calaveras Grove, where he found a huge tree. After returning to camp, he made up a tale of a big grizzly and invited anyone interested to come with him to see it. Of course, the tree was the real center of interest.[4] Soon this tree was gleefully whacked down and the top of the stump was used as a dance floor.[5] Another tree, "The Mother of the Forest" was skinned of its bark. The tree soon died and the bark was displayed at the Crystal Palace in London.[6] It is possible that someone named Wooster was in the grove in 1850. He supposedly carved his name and date on the Hercules Tree, which fell in 1861. It was a pretty big tree.

The Mariposa Grove, now in Yosemite National Park, may have been discovered in 1850 by Major Burney. In 1857, Galen Clark built a cabin in the grove and sought to publicize the area.[7] Giant Forest, now part of Sequoia National Park, was shown to cattleman Hale Tharp in 1856 by local Indians.[8] It wasn't long before most of the larger groves were known. It is interesting to note that several relatively small groves of sequoias have been identified only recently.

Early pioneers were awed by the immense giant sequoia. Photograph from NPS collection, Sequoia National Park.

Since these first discoveries, the size of these trees has been a source of amazement. As sequoia groves were discovered, new champions were proclaimed by local enthusiasts. Trees were measured with string, lariats, rifles, and boot lengths. It is not surprising that measurements were often exaggerated and that jealousies abounded. Exaggerations are still found in some publications.

The peak of interest and rivalry came in the 1920s. In order to settle the question of which tree was the biggest, the Fresno Junior Chamber of Commerce selected a team of engineers, called here the "Jourdan Team," after its chairman, J. W. Jourdan, to measure four contenders. They selected two from Fresno County, the General Grant (Grant Grove) and the Boole Tree (Converse Basin). Two trees were selected from Tulare County, the General Sherman (Giant Forest) and the Hart Tree (Redwood Mountain Grove). For some strange reason they selected the Hart Tree even though there were at least three trees in Giant Forest that were obviously larger. My guess is that politics were involved. At that time the Redwood Mountain Grove was in private hands, but there was a strong interest in having this grove added to the National Park System. What better way than to have a champion tree in this grove! Someone reported a really big tree, three times as large as the General Sherman. The Hart certainly does not live up to its reputation.[9]

Early measurements of the giant sequoia were often highly inaccurate. Since no standard had been established, the diameter measurement of a tree would vary greatly depending on who did the measuring. The Jourdan Team established excellent standards for determining size.[10] In my measurements, I generally follow their lead. Now would be a good time to turn to Appendix I, *Measurement Terms*.

The Jourdan Team determined that the four trees they measured ranked as follows: 1) General Sherman, 2) General Grant, 3) Boole, and 4) Hart. Mr. N. E. Beckwith, a member of the Jourdan Team, thought the wrong trees had been measured. He promptly measured the Lincoln and the President in Giant Forest and declared the Lincoln larger than the Sherman, with the President third largest. Apparently Colonel White, then superintendent of Sequoia National Park, did not exactly jump up and down with great enthusiasm when he heard this news, since the new parking area near the Sherman had just been completed and he was not about to run a new road to the Lincoln Tree. A note to his staff said not to blab about the Lincoln.[11]

Wendell Flint in Giant Forest in 1950.

Personal History

If there was one major reason for my initial interest in really big sequoias, it was snoring. After graduating from the University of California at Berkeley, I found myself assigned to a tank battalion in Word War II and cooped up with dozens of snorers. When my military stint ended, seeking peaceful nights, I pitched my tent in Giant Forest in Sequoia National Park. To fill the days, I started to look closely at the more famous trees. I concluded something was awry. For example, I discovered that the McKinley Tree was not 28 feet in diameter as proclaimed, but 22 feet at ground level.[12] I borrowed a transit and measured the Washington Tree and found it to be as large as the General Grant Tree – number two according to the literature. I have been looking for big ones ever since! I have found the older data on the giant sequoias to include many incorrect measurements.

My primary partner on my search for the world's largest trees, was Mike Law, who contributed greatly to this book. He has taken nearly all the photographs and assisted on measuring treks. He provided a lot of the dirty work in correctly locating transit points. I met Mike in 1952 while camped at the Long Meadow Grove. He was 12 years old at the time. I was invited to the Law family campfire, where I prattled about Big Trees and Mr. Law expounded on fish. Years later, Mike got the urge to do some sequoia photography. Fortunately, his dad remembered my name and where I was from. Since 1969 we have been hunting the big ones together.

Mike Law (center) poses in front of a giant sequoia in 1952 with his dad, Richard and brother Dennis.

How to Get Fooled While Looking for a Giant

Mike and I have spent countless hours hiking to trees that shrank to pure insignificance when we got close. Here are some illusions that plagued us.

Big Base Illusion: Early viewers fell for this with great regularity. To be really big, a tree must be large high on the trunk. Some trees with a large base taper too much to be contenders. I doubt if many old-timers carried a transit or laser, so I cannot be too harsh on them.

Double Tree Illusion: What appears to be a really big one is actually two trees lined up to appear from a distance to be a single tree.

Flattened Base Illusion: Some trees are flattened by fire and seem smaller than they are. The General Grant has a base that is 40.3 feet in diameter one way, but only 27 feet across the other.

Surroundings Illusion: A big one appears smaller if it is but one in a group of many large specimens, or may seem huge if there are only small trees surrounding it.

Uphill Illusion: Trees on a hill seem much larger when viewed from below.

How Do Other Large Trees Compare?

A determination of which tree is the largest is based on overall volume, not by diameter or height. Only the coast redwood (*Sequoia sempervirens*) is in the race for the largest tree. There have been tales of several coast redwoods larger than the General Sherman Tree, but these trees have fallen or have been cut down.

There is a huge Montezuma bald cypress near Oaxaca, Mexico, which has an enormous

Photographer Mike Law.

base, larger than any sequoia. It appears to be at least three trees fused together, although some maintain it is one. The largest bald cypress reaches a maximum height only half that of the largest giant sequoia. The Kauri in New Zealand are impressive, but generally much shorter. The largest is 45 feet around, but only 169 feet in height with a volume of less than 9,000 cubic feet. One was supposed to contain 30,000 cubic feet in trunk volume, but it fell years ago.[13] The Japanese Cryptomeria with its 20 to 30 foot diameter, rivals the sequoia, but it only grows to 125 feet in height. The African baobob has a diameter that also rivals the sequoia, but only reaches a height of 60 feet.

In the Western United States, there are several very large species:

Western red cedar (*Thuja plicata*)
Known to exceed 200 feet in height. The greatest known trunk volume is about 14,500 cubic feet. These trees range from Northern California to Alaska.

Douglas fir (*Pseudotsuga menziezii*)
This tree can have a breast height diameter of over 15 feet, be over 325 feet tall and have a trunk volume up to 13,500 cubic feet. It ranges from Northern California into Canada.

Sitka spruce (*Picea sitchensis*)
This tree can have a breast height diameter of up to 18.7 feet and a height of up to 315 feet. It ranges from Northern California to Alaska and into the Rocky Mountains.

Sugar pine (*Pinus lambertiana*)
This tree can reach 10 feet in diameter at breast height and can sometimes exceed 250 feet in height with a trunk volume of 10,000 cubic feet. It ranges from Oregon to Baja California, Mexico.

How Big is a Giant Sequoia?

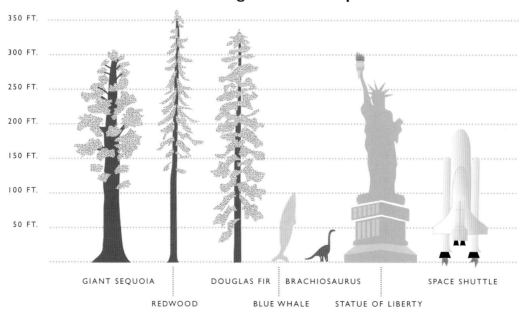

350 FT.
300 FT.
250 FT.
200 FT.
150 FT.
100 FT.
50 FT.

GIANT SEQUOIA   DOUGLAS FIR   BRACHIOSAURUS   SPACE SHUTTLE

REDWOOD   BLUE WHALE   STATUE OF LIBERTY

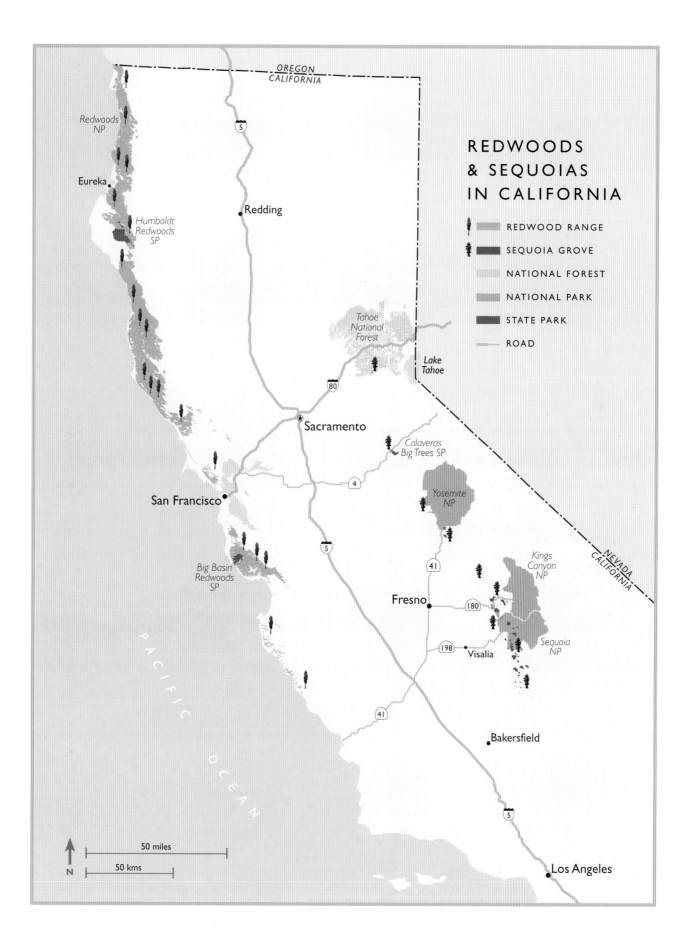

OREGON
CALIFORNIA

Redwoods NP

Eureka

Humboldt Redwoods SP

Redding

Tahoe National Forest

Lake Tahoe

REDWOODS & SEQUOIAS IN CALIFORNIA

REDWOOD RANGE
SEQUOIA GROVE
NATIONAL FOREST
NATIONAL PARK
STATE PARK
ROAD

Sacramento

Calaveras Big Trees SP

Yosemite NP

San Francisco

Big Basin Redwoods SP

Fresno

Kings Canyon NP

Visalia

Sequoia NP

NEVADA
CALIFORNIA

Bakersfield

PACIFIC OCEAN

50 miles

50 kms

N

Los Angeles

Wendell Flint at the Discovery Stump.

Chapter 2:

GROVES NORTH
OF THE KINGS RIVER

North of the Kings River watershed are eight giant sequoia groves that are relatively small and isolated from the large groves to the south. There are at least four giants with trunk volumes over 30,000 cubic feet. These trees were among the first big ones discovered.

North and South Calaveras Groves

These two groves, located in Calaveras Big Trees State Park, are about six miles apart. The North Grove, covering about 60 acres, is on a small creek – Big Trees Creek. The South Grove, about 445 acres, is on Beaver Creek.[1] Highway 4 from Highway 99 at the south end of Stockton reaches the park and the North Grove. From there, the South Grove may be reached by means of a good trail. Augustus Dowd found the North Calaveras Grove in 1862.[2] The South Calaveras Grove was found soon after.

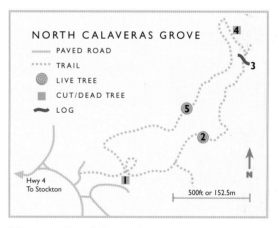

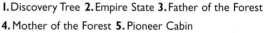

1. Discovery Tree **2.** Empire State **3.** Father of the Forest
4. Mother of the Forest **5.** Pioneer Cabin

Things to See in the North Calaveras Grove
There is no doubt that the North Calaveras Grove, which is loaded with sequoia history, once contained some trees of remarkable size.

Discovery Tree (#1 NC)
One of the first things on the self-guided trail is the stump of the Discovery Tree. This stump is about 24 feet across without bark or sapwood, and was supposed to be a little over 300 feet high when standing. It took 22 days with augers and wedges to fell this 1,224-year-old tree. What is left of the trunk indicates it was not a rival for the really big ones. The stump was smoothed for use as a dancehall with a bowling alley placed atop the horizontal trunk.

Apparently Mr. Dowd, its discoverer, was not pleased with its felling.

Empire State Tree (#2 NC)

The Empire State, which leans a bit, is the North Calaveras Grove's largest living tree, measuring 19.5 feet in diameter at breast height and 217 feet tall.

Father of the Forest (#3 NC)

A hollow log is all that remains of a large tree that fell before the grove was discovered. It was said to be 110 feet around and over 400 feet tall. I don't think so.

Mother of the Forest (#4 NC)

Another great tree, possibly the grove's largest, was killed when its bark was stripped off to be displayed at the Crystal Palace in London. According to Hartesveldt et al. 1975, it originally had a base diameter of 31 feet. It was said to be over 300 feet tall. One totally ridiculous figure said it was 362 feet tall. Our forebears exaggerated a lot.

Pioneer Cabin (#5 NC)

This tree has a wide base with a road cut through it in emulation of the famous Wawona tunneled tree in the Mariposa Grove of Yosemite. The tree is almost dead, likely the result of someone cutting a hole through it. Walking through it gives a good sense of the size of a giant sequoia. It is about 22 feet wide at the road cut.

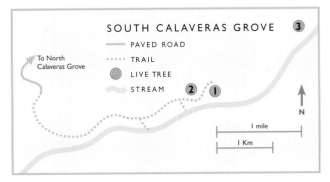

1. Agassiz 2. Palace Hotel 3. Smith Cabin

Notable Sequoias in the South Calaveras Grove

Although there are a number of impressive trees in this grove, only one is known to rank among the largest.

Louis Agassiz Tree (#1 SC)

Named after a Swiss-American zoologist and geologist (1807-73), it is one of the few trees named for a scientist, rather than a general or out of personal pride. For a time it was considered one of the largest. This is not the case, but it is impressive and worth seeing. The tree has a vast cavity burned on the south side, hollowing out the tree to a height of about 70 feet. It is on an extension of the loop trail through the South Calaveras Grove, about 2.5 miles from the trailhead.

Mike and I measured this tree in 1974 with a rather poor transit. The diameters I obtained may be 2 inches off either way. I have a feeling the measurements taken are too small. In 1998,

Dr. Robert Van Pelt measured the height at 262 feet with a laser instrument.[3] The Evans survey, using an unreliable instrument, the hypsometer, gave it 250 feet.[4] In 1974, I measured 243.3 feet. In looking over my data, I discovered a very dubious procedure, so I am tossing out my height data.

Agassiz Tree dimensions:		
	ENGLISH	METRIC
Height	262.0 feet	79.85 meters
GROUND PERIMETER	97.0	29.56
DIAMETER: AT BREAST HIGH	22.3	6.80
AT 60 FEET/18.3 M	12.9	3.93
AT 120 FEET/36.6 M	12.7	3.87
AT 180 FEET/54.9 M	10.0	3.05
VOLUME IGNORING BURNS	30,580 cubic feet	866 cubic meters

Palace Hotel (#2 SC)

This tree has a huge hollowed out base due to fire, but is of no great size higher up. The Evans Cruise list says it has a diameter breast high of 21.4 feet, a diameter of 14.5 feet at 16 feet and a height of 290 feet, but I do not trust the height measurements.[5]

Smith Cabin (#3 SC)

This tree has been touted as a rival of the Agassiz, but Dr. Van Pelt and friends visited the tree in 1998 and found that although it has a huge base, it is small above. The 1924 Evans data shows it as having a breast high diameter of 20.8 feet, a diameter of 17.7 feet at 16 feet and a height of 270 feet. This tree is off the trail near the eastern edge of the grove.[6]

Tuolumne Grove

This 16-acre grove in Yosemite National Park is reached by going one mile north of the Crane Flat Ranger Station and taking the one-way Old Big Oak Flat Road. Although no really Big Trees exist here today, there are the remains of two, the Dead Giant on a spur road and the King of the Forest. The Dead Giant was tunneled in 1878 so it could be driven through. It was 29.5 feet through the base, and had a 20.8 feet diameter breast high as measured by Dion in 1966.[7]

The King of the Forest is a much-reduced tree. The upper trunk is gone, but a new leader is

growing. In 1930, Bellue measured it at 103 feet around at ground level.[8] A breast high diameter of 26.4 feet was measured by Dion in 1966. This could have been a big one.

The Outstanding Mariposa Grove

This very interesting grove is on the southern border of Yosemite National Park. The 250-acre grove is reached by a paved road just past the park's south entrance on Highway 41. It is one of the earlier known groves, first publicized in 1857. It may have been discovered as early as 1849.[9] It has two trees of remarkable size and the remains of at least two more that were of great size when standing.

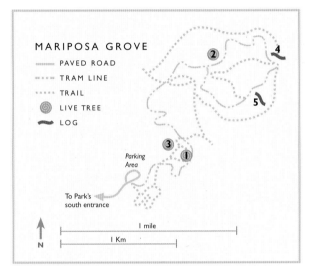

1. Grizzly Giant 2. Washington 3. California
4. Wawona Log 5. Massachusetts Log

Grizzly Giant (#1 MG)

Wow – what a sight! This is a tree that any giant sequoia aficionado must see. It may not be the largest tree in the grove, but it clearly is the most spectacular. It leans from the vertical by as much as 18 feet at the top, making the tree appear like it is about to topple –though its center of gravity is above the massive base.

It has many great limbs, some 6 feet in diameter. It is a stubby tree at 209 feet high, but this, as well as a large basal buttress on one side, seems to accent its bulk. Mason Hutchings named the tree the "Grizzled Giant" in 1859 at the suggestion of Galen Clark. The name was soon altered to "Grizzly Giant."

This tree has been measured several times, the most definitively in 1932 by a team supervised by A. E. Cowell, an engineer appointed by Park Superintendent Thompson. To find out how much the tree had grown in 58 years, Mike Law, John Hawksworth and I tried to measure the tree again in 1990 using the transit points described by Cowell in his report. Unfortunately, only two transit points were recoverable and even those were approximate, but the results compared very well. The only figure that doesn't quite agree is the diameter at 180 feet. At that height, the trunk is very irregular and we were unable to recover Cowell's original transit points.

Grizzly Giant dimensions:				
	FLINT (1990):		COWELL (1932):	
	ENGLISH	METRIC	ENGLISH	METRIC
HEIGHT	209.0 feet*	63.70 meters*	209.0 feet	63.70 meters
GROUND PERIMETER	92.5	28.19	96.5	29.41
DIAMETER: AT BREAST HIGH	25.4	7.74	not available	
AT 60 FEET/18.3 M	16.3	4.97	15.8	4.82
AT 120 FEET/36.6 M	13.4	4.08	13.2	4.02
AT 180 FEET/54.9 M	5.7	1.74	6.1	1.86
VOLUME IGNORING BURNS	34,005 cu. feet	963 cu. meters	30,300 cu. feet	858 cu. meters
* Cowell data				

Washington Tree (#2 MG)

The early measurements taken on the Washington show that it is a rival to the Grizzly Giant. In 1990 Mike Law, John Hawksworth, and I went to Yosemite to find out how big it really is. It turns out that the Grizzly Giant is just a bit smaller than the less inspiring Washington.

Washington Tree dimensions:		
	ENGLISH	METRIC
HEIGHT	236.0 feet	71.93 meters
GROUND PERIMETER	95.7	29.17
DIAMETER: AT BREAST HIGH	23.8	7.25
AT 60 FEET/18.3 M	15.1	4.60
AT 120 FEET/36.6 M	13.1	3.99
AT 180 FEET/54.9 M	10.5	3.20
VOLUME IGNORING BURNS	35,901 cubic feet	1,016 cubic meters

California (#3 MG)

This still-standing tree near the Grizzly Giant has an old road through it. The road was cut so that in winter, when the Wawona could not be accessed due to snow, visitors could be duped into thinking they had seen the famous Wawona Tree.

Wawona (#4 MG)

The famous Wawona Tree fell during the winter of 1968-69. The Wawona had a road cut through it in 1881. It was in the 30,000 cubic foot category, 234 feet tall and 26 feet wide

The famous Wawona Tree. Photograph from National Park Service Collection, Yosemite National Park.

through the tunnel.

Massachusetts (#5 MG)

This tree fell in 1927. It was about 28 feet across at ground level. I measured a 14-foot diameter approximately 40 feet from the bottom of the trunk.

Forest Giant

No longer standing, this giant was on fire when it was first discovered. It was supposed to be 34 feet in diameter at breast height. In the 1990s, Stan Hutchinson, a student of the northern sequoia groves, located what little remains of this once mighty tree. This is not on the map because there is virtually nothing to see.[10]

Nelder Grove

The Nelder Grove lies about four miles south of the Mariposa, mostly on Sierra National Forest land. It is really a complex of groves, some of which are fairly well separated. The main units lie along California Creek, Nelder Ridge, Upper Nelder Creek, and Basin and Lower Nelder Creek. The grove can be reached by taking Highway 41 to the Sky Ranch Road on the

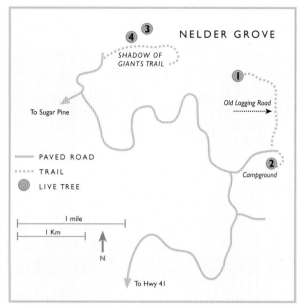

NELDER GROVE

SHADOW OF GIANTS TRAIL

To Sugar Pine

Old Logging Road

Campground

PAVED ROAD
TRAIL
LIVE TREE

1 mile
1 Km

N

To Hwy 41

1. Nelder 2. Bull Buck 3. Millikan 4. Upside-Down Tree

east side of Highway 41, then north on Road 6S90 to the grove. It was heavily logged of sequoias after 1874, but 108 mature giants remain.

Nelder Tree (#1 NG)

John Muir saw this tree in 1875. John A. Nelder had a camp near the tree and told Muir it was the world's largest tree. Muir measured it at 26 feet in diameter, probably at ground level. Nelder was a bit put out when Muir told him there was a bigger tree in the Mariposa Grove – the Grizzly Giant.

The Nelder Tree is not on a regular trail, but can be seen by leaving the campground near the Bull Buck Tree, following an old logging road along California Creek for less than a mile, and then bushwhacking westward staying near boggy areas. This tree is the second largest standing sequoia north of the Kings River. The lower trunk is nearly cylindrical for the first 90 feet and then tapers gradually to the top. John Hawksworth, Stan Hutchinson, Mike Law and I made some measurements in 1986. John, Mike and I finished the job in 1989.

	Nelder Tree dimensions:	
	ENGLISH	METRIC
HEIGHT	266.2 feet	81.13 meters
GROUND PERIMETER	90.0	27.43
DIAMETER: AT BREAST HIGH	21.0	6.40
AT 60 FEET/18.3 M	14.8	4.51
AT 120 FEET/36.6 M	14.0	4.27
AT 180 FEET/54.9 M	10.3	3.14
VOLUME IGNORING BURNS	34,993 cubic feet	991 cubic meters

The Bull Buck Fiasco (#2 NG)

In 1975, the Bull Buck was measured under the sponsorship of the American Forestry Association. It was rated by a point system that works well on much smaller trees in the

Eastern United States. The rating system adds the perimeter at 4.5 feet (above ground level) in inches, the height in feet, and one-quarter of the average crown spread in feet. The Bull Buck earned 1,275 points. The General Sherman was worth 1,300 points - a virtual tie! However, when trunk volumes are compared, the Sherman is almost twice as large as the Bull Buck. I recall giggling a little bit when I first saw this "rival" of the Sherman. The Bull Buck has an enormous base. But the trunk above the base is rather puny. If you remember not to look up, it can give the impression of great size.

Bull Buck measurements by the American Forestry Association:		
	ENGLISH	METRIC
HEIGHT	246.1 feet	75.01 meters
GROUND PERIMETER	99.1	30.20
DIAMETER AT BREAST HIGH	26.8	8.17
LINE B AT 34 FEET/10.4 M	13.4	4.08
LINE C AT 115 FEET/351 M	11.7	3.57
LINE C AT 170 FEET/51.8 M	8.9	2.71
VOLUME (IGNORING BURNS)	27,383 cubic feet	775 cubic meters
Lines B and C are approximately 90 degrees apart (AFA Assn. Report on Sherman vs. Bull Buck).		

Millikan Tree (#3 NG)

The large Millikan, located on California Institute of Technology land on the ridge top above the Shadow of the Giants Trail, is approximately 20 feet in diameter at breast height and has a heavy lower trunk. It has not been adequately measured.

Upside Down Tree (#4 NG)

This strange tree looks as if it had been inverted so that the roots are on top. This illusion results from its abnormal growth from knots near the top.

Forest King

This tree, located east of the Nelder Tree in the California Creek watershed, was felled by undercutting in 1870 for an exhibition. John Hawksworth and Stan Hutchinson studied the parts that are left. It was said to be 34 feet in diameter at an unstated height. Another source quotes an 1871 magazine article claiming the diameter to be 40 feet and 4 inches.[11] Stan tells me that the tree partially righted itself when some roots were cut through. This may have been the source of several rumors about a huge tree to the north of General Grant. There was a rumor that there was an undocumented grove east of the Nelder Grove. Bob Rogers of the Forest Service assures me it does not exist.

The General Grant Tree.

Chapter 3:

THE KINGS RIVER GROVES

The Kings River watershed has some very large sequoias, several remnants of huge trees, and acres of giant sequoias that have been felled. The large Converse Basin Grove has just a few small areas left uncut. The Indian Basin Grove was completely logged. The northwestern part of the Evans Grove has only a few mature trees left and the Big Stump Grove, except for a few big trees, was completely cut down. A small part of the Grant Grove that is outside of Kings Canyon National Park is devoid of any giants. However, there are beautiful sequoia forests still standing.

Grant and Big Stump Groves in Kings Canyon National Park

There are three groves in the western portion of Kings Canyon National Park. The fabulous Grant Grove, covering about 154 acres in the park and as much as 30 cut-over acres in the Giant Sequoia National Monument, has many very large trees and is easy to access. From Fresno, follow Highway 180 through the national park entrance gate at the edge of the Big Stump Grove. About one mile up, take the left fork in the road. In another mile and just past the visitor center, there is a sign for the road to the Grant Tree. The Big Stump Grove covers 257 acres in the park and about 380 acres in the Giant Sequoia National Monument. Located mostly within the park, the small Sequoia Creek Grove contains the South King Tree, which is 21 feet in diameter at breast height.

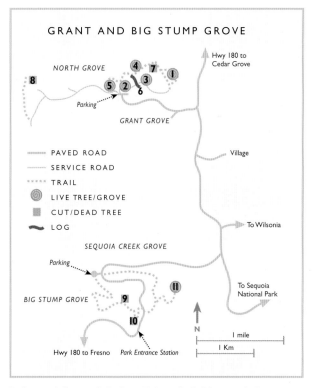

1. General Grant 2. Robert E. Lee 3. California 4. Oregon 5. Lincoln 6. Fallen Monarch 7. Centennial Stump 8. Dead Giant 9. Burnt Monarch 10. Mark Twain 11. Sawed Tree

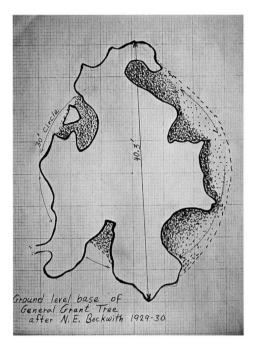

Map of the base of the General Grant.

General Grant Tree (#1 GB)

There is some argument as to how and when this tree was named. Generally accepted is the story that it was found by Joseph Hardin Thomas in 1862 and named by Lucretia Baker of Visalia in 1867. However, Mr. Thomas, the owner of a local sawmill, said that he was the one who really named the tree. When Hudson D. Barton measured the ground perimeter in 1866, he said that it was already called the General Grant. In 1926 it was designated as the Nation's Christmas Tree and services are held annually.[1]

Until 1931, it was often considered the world's largest tree, with its main rivals being the General Sherman and the Boole. The Jourdan Team rated it as the second largest. Mike Law and I measured it again in 1976 for the American Forestry Association, and the data agreed quite well. The Washington Tree in Giant Forest has a greater volume if the burns are ignored. The Grant may have a slightly greater mass. Only extensive measurements of the burned areas could settle which one is number two.

The Grant is very imposing. The eastern side has a huge burn leaving the lower trunk very flattened, giving the tree a maximum base diameter on the ground of 40.3 feet in the wide direction but only 27 feet in the other direction. Part of this large basal diameter can be attributed to a huge buttress on the north side.

General Grant Tree dimensions (1976 measurements):		
	ENGLISH	METRIC
HEIGHT	268.1 feet	81.71 meters
GROUND PERIMETER	107.5	32.76
DIAMETER: AT BREAST HIGH	28.9	8.81
AT 60 FEET/18.3 M	16.3	4.97
AT 120 FEET/36.6 M	15.0	4.57
AT 180 FEET/54.9 M	12.9	3.93
VOLUME IGNORING BURNS	46,608 cubic feet	1,320 cubic meters

While measuring this tree, an onlooker inquired when we were going to climb it to get the height. We told him that we had a better way. We would tie a string to a squirrel's tail, toss an acorn over the top and send the little beast after it. Then we would measure the string. The Castro Tree in the Redwood Mountain Grove and others have been measured by dropping a tape from the top by climbing the tree!

Robert E. Lee.

Robert E. Lee (#2 GB)

Richard Field, a Confederate lieutenant, named this tree, probably in 1875.[2] Mike Law and I ignored this tree for years. The huge Grant Tree simply dwarfed the Lee. We finally got around to measuring it in 1985, and to our surprise, it was the 12th largest we had measured. It does not have the overwhelming base of the Grant, but the trunk does not taper much. A basal buttress on the tree's west side affects the breast height measurement. If the buttress is excluded, the breast high diameter is 22 feet. My data include the buttress. This is a fine specimen – don't pass it by.

Robert E. Lee dimensions:		
	ENGLISH	METRIC
HEIGHT	254.7 feet	77.63 meters
GROUND PERIMETER	88.3	26.91
DIAMETER: AT BREAST HIGH	23.8	7.25
AT 60 FEET/18.3 M	16.5	5.03
AT 120 FEET/36.6 M	14.4	4.39
AT 180 FEET/54.9 M	11.2	3.41
VOLUME IGNORING BURNS	40,102 cubic feet	1,135 cubic meters

Other Wonderful Nearby Sequoia Sights

California, Oregon, Lincoln (#3, #4, #5 GB)

The California was once taller, but a lightning fire in 1967 reduced the height by about 25 feet. The tree was actually climbed to put out the fire. The Oregon lost a huge limb a few years ago, which can be seen nearby. The Lincoln Tree has a large base, but tapers too much to be eligible for my list of big ones. There is a larger tree, also named Lincoln, in Giant Forest.

Notable Dead Trees in the Grant Grove Area

Fallen Monarch (#6 GB)

The Gamlin brothers lived in this huge hollow log until they built a nearby cabin. This log was later used as a stable and as a place to guzzle hooch.

Centennial Stump (#7 GB)

This is the remains of a large sequoia that was illegally cut down for the Exposition of Philadelphia in 1875[3]. It measures 24 feet across at the cut.

Dead Giant (#8 GB)

This dead snag is near the western edge of the grove near the park boundary. It appears to have been killed by girdling, for what reason I don't know.

Burnt Monarch or Old Adam (#9 GB)

This big snag is in the Big Stump Grove. There is parking just north of the park's entrance station and a trail leads to the Burnt Monarch and the Mark Twain Stump. The Burnt Monarch could have been one of the largest when it was alive. This dead tree has been known since the early 1880s when this area was being logged of nearly all sequoias. The Burnt Monarch has a ground perimeter of 97.8 feet and a breast high diameter of 25.7 feet – and this with no deep burns and bark!

Mark Twain Stump (# 10 GB)

This tree was cut in 1891 at the request of the American Museum of Natural History. Its present ground perimeter is 86 feet, and its diameter across the stump measures 24 feet.

Felling the Mark Twain. Photograph from NPS collection, Sequoia National Park.

THE KING RIVER GROVES

23

Sawed Tree (#11 GB)

This tree was nearly cut through, but it didn't tumble when it should have, so the loggers became a bit upset and went away. Though it has shifted a bit on its stump, it is still healthy.

Converse Basin – The Great Devastated Grove

Converse Basin is north of the General Grant area on Highway 180 just past Cherry Gap. Forest Service Road 13S03 goes to the Chicago Stump and Forest Service Road 13S55 goes to the Muir Snag, Stump Meadow, and the trailhead for the Boole Tree. Both are dirt roads. This large grove in the Giant Sequoia National Monument covers 3,500 acres and was nearly logged of all sequoias between 1892 and 1918. Just a few old growth trees remain, perhaps 60 large ones out of thousands. There are lots of second growth sequoias, some beginning to look like mature trees. Some of the trees near the Chicago Stump exceeded 3,000 years old when cut.

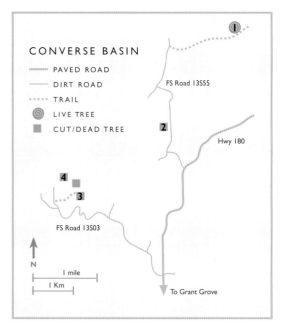

CONVERSE BASIN
- PAVED ROAD
- DIRT ROAD
- TRAIL
- LIVE TREE
- CUT/DEAD TREE

FS Road 13S55
Hwy 180
FS Road 13S03
N
1 mile
1 Km
To Grant Grove

1. Boole 2. Muir Snag 3. Chicago Stump
4. D25 Stump

Boole Tree (#1 CB)

A three-quarters of a mile-long trail leads to the Boole. The trailhead is found by turning north from Stump Meadow to where Forest Service Road 13S55 ends. The tree was named around 1895 by A. H. Sweeny, a Fresno doctor, after Frank A. Boole, supervisor of the logging operation. It was originally thought to be the largest tree. However, it was the third largest after the Sherman and Grant as determined by the Jourdan Team.[4] I rate it number seven.

At the Boole Tree in 1980. (l to r) Jerry Latham, Becky Law, Jim Warner, unknown participant, Wendell Flint.

Boole Tree. Photograph by Dick Burns.

In 1980, Mike Law, his young daughter Becky, Jerry Latham, park naturalist Jim Warner and I measured this tree utilizing the older data. We agreed with the 1931 Jourdan Team data. Becky volunteered to carry the transit, but since the old transit weighed as much as she, she took one step and gave up.

Boole Tree dimensions:		
	ENGLISH	METRIC
HEIGHT	268.8 feet	81.93 meters
GROUND PERIMETER	113.0	34.44
DIAMETER:AT BREAST HIGH	25.4	7.74
AT 60 FEET/18.3 M	15.6	4.75
AT 120 FEET/36.6 M	13.7	4.18
AT 180 FEET/54.9 M	11.7	3.57
VOLUME IGNORING BURNS	42,472 cubic feet	1,202 cubic meters

Muir Snag (#2 CB)

The Muir Snag is near Forest Service Road 13S55. A short trail leads to this remnant of a truly monstrous tree. Native Americans guided John Muir to this tree in 1875. The snag is nearly burned in half. By clearing charcoal from the hollow center of the tree, Muir counted 4,000 growth rings. This tree was "lost" until Bob Walker found it in 1976. Walker, park naturalist Dale Schmidt, and I made measurements. The tree fit Muir's description very closely indeed. I made a map of its base and obtained some perimeters by tape.

Muir's age estimate cannot be confirmed. I found that he had counted some rings he should not have. One of the cavities loops back toward the center of the tree, causing Muir to count some rings more than once. Muir said the tree had a near base diameter of 35 feet 8 inches and was about 140 feet tall. Everything matched. I found a maximum base diameter on the level of 35.2 feet in 1976 and 35.9 feet in 1983 (the base was somewhat disturbed by nearby logging). I was able to count 2,250 rings. I extrapolated my data to arrive at an age of 3,000 to 3,500 years. Increment borings by Dr. Tom Harvey of San Jose State University gave an age of 2,625 years. Dr. Harvey's estimation is probably too low because of the location of the borings. He actually thought the tree could be over 3,000 years old.[5] I measured the snag to be 133 feet tall. Before being partially burned away, the base perimeter could have been as much as 107 feet.

Chicago Stump (#3 CB)

The Chicago Stump, called the General Noble before it was cut, is on a short trail reached by taking Forest Service Road 13S03, which leaves Highway 180 just north of Cherry Gap. From Forest Service Road 13S03, take Forest Service Road 13S66 to the trail.

This is the remains of a great sequoia that was cut to be exhibited at the World's Columbian Exposition (The Chicago World's Fair) in 1892. Its bark was reassembled to look a little like the tree. People who saw this exhibit tended to snicker and declare it to be one of those western fakes. Later, the U. S. Navy, into whose care it had been given, lost the whole thing. The remaining stump has a ground perimeter of about 96 feet and is about 16.5 feet by 19.3 feet in diameter at the cut, which is about 20 feet above the ground. The old stump has been somewhat reduced by fire since 1975.

Dr. Donald J. McGraw was kind enough to send me copies of his work on the history of this tree.[6] From the pictures, I concluded that it was probably smaller than the General Sherman. It was supposedly 285 feet tall.

D25 Stump (#4 CB)

One hundred yards north of the Chicago Stump, the D25 has a ring count of nearly 3,126, indicating that it was that old when cut a century ago. It was not a huge tree, perhaps 17 feet in diameter at the cut. A nearby stump was found to have about a hundred more rings.

Evans Complex of Groves

This vast area of giant sequoias consists of at least eight groves, some only narrowly separated. A large part of the Evans Grove and one unit of the Lockwood Grove have been logged of sequoias. There are two trees in this area that qualify as big ones.

Evans Tree (#1 EC)

This tree, which I call the Evans Tree, is in the Evans Grove. It is reached by turning north at Quail Flat on the Generals Highway, then going eastward almost immediately on Forest Service Road 14S02 to Road 13S26, and finally to Road 13S05. The last two or three miles are probably not drivable, and likely must be done on foot. The road splits near the end and the right branch heads south towards Evans Creek

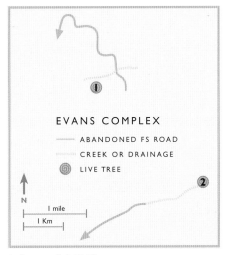

1. Evans   2. Ishi Giant

drainage. The tree is uphill to the southwest several hundred yards. It is easy to miss. This tree is remarkable in that it is so undercut by fire that the measurements at the base are surprisingly small. It has a pronounced lean downhill and a very heavy trunk above the burned areas. Mike and I noted this tree in 1980, and Keith Hintergardt, Ed Kreyenhagen, and I measured it in 1981.

Evans Tree dimensions:		
	ENGLISH	METRIC
HEIGHT	232.4 feet	70.83 meters
GROUND PERIMETER	77.5	23.62
DIAMETER:AT BREAST HIGH	17.7	5.39
AT 60 FEET/18.3 M	15.6	4.75
AT 120 FEET/36.6 M	13.7	4.18
AT 180 FEET/54.9 M	7.0	2.13
VOLUME IGNORING BURNS	30,232 cubic feet	856 cubic meters

Ishi Giant (#2 EC)

Dwight Willard, author of *Giant Sequoia Groves of the Sierra Nevada*, was doing some giant sequoia hunting in 1993 when he came across a remarkably large tree in the Kennedy Grove. Some sources call this the Burton Grove. Here is a tree whose massive base rivals the General Sherman. It is badly burned, and as a result has two flying buttresses, one very thin and fragile. The Ishi is an average height tree with a very heavy lower trunk.

Later that year Bob Rogers, Dwight Willard, Mike Law, and I measured the tree. It was a bit unnerving to find a skull in front of the tree. I thought it was fitting to call Dwight's find the Calavera Tree, calavera being Spanish for skull. Dwight would have nothing of that, and proposed the "Ishi Giant." Ishi was the last remaining member of the Yahi Tribe of the Mount Lassen area. He died in 1916.

We measured the tree a little differently since we had a laser device. One line was done the usual way with a transit and tape. The second line used the laser to get heights and distances and provided a direct way of getting diameters by measuring the width of the shadow. Normally, this method gives only an approximation because the heights are guesses. We obtained results that were in agreement with the measurements taken on the other line using the transit. The laser was also used to get its height from a number of spots. I did not supervise this as I was taking other measurements. The height figures were too short and not consistent.

The Ishi Giant with discoverer Dwight Willard (left) and Bob Rogers.

Later I surmised that the distance to the tree had not included the distance from the outer edge to the axis of the tree. I got consistent results when I took this into account. I would like to measure the height again using a transit.

In 1993, it was easy to walk to the tree. The road to the edge of the grove is now in very bad condition, so it is a moderately long walk. In order to get to the edge of the grove, take Forest Service Road 14S02 at Quail Flat for about 12 miles, then turn eastward on the Little Boulder Creek Road 13S23 that skirts the Little Boulder Grove. You may be able to drive part of this road if you don't mind scratches on your vehicle. The last part will probably be impassable. From there, it is cross-country about a mile to the grove's southeast corner.

We definitely were not the first to see the tree. There were carvings, some dating back to 1940. The mystery of the skull was finally solved. It seems some teenagers went into the grove and did not get out.[7] No remains other than the one skull were ever found.

The ground perimeter measurement needs a little explaining. There is a large root-like structure on the south side of the tree that merges with the main trunk, so the level of the tape is arbitrary. For measuring purposes, I simply took what looked like tree bole rather than root. There are also two remnants of the original trunk on the west side of the tree. I measured around those. The following measurements are a composite of my 1993 measurements and new measurements by Dr. Van Pelt using a laser instrument in the late 1990s.

Ishi Giant dimensions:		
	ENGLISH	METRIC
HEIGHT	255.0 feet	77.72 meters
GROUND PERIMETER	105.1	32.03
DIAMETER: AT BREAST HIGH	25.5	7.77
AT 60 FEET/18.3 M	15.5	4.72
AT 120 FEET/36.6 M	13.1	3.99
AT 180 FEET/54.9 M	10.5	3.20
VOLUME (IGNORING BURNS)	38,156 cubic feet	1,080 cubic meters

Rumors

Forest Clingan of Dunlap, California, a great admirer of all that relates to sequoias, sent me an interesting clipping from 1890.[8] It tells of mountaineer Frank Lewis of Sanger, California, who chased a large brown bear to a point about two miles north of Kennedy Meadow. Early Big

Tree reporters liked chasing bears. Lewis found a tree, which he measured at 129 feet 5 inches around at 4 feet above the ground with a rope that he had to go back to Kennedy Meadow to get. Mr. Lewis offered to take anyone in to see his monster tree. I have found no record that anyone did.

If Lewis' directions were correct, this would put his tree in the Camp 7 area of the Evans Grove. The nearest large tree I could find in this area is the Evans Tree, which is big, though I doubt it could ever have been as large as Lewis' tree. I found no stump that would account for this tree. Mike and I did spot a broken tree south of the Evans Tree that seemed to have a very heavy lower trunk. We have not looked at it close up, and we did not go to it because it obviously was very short. Perhaps Mr. Lewis had something other than water in his canteen. Assuming his directions were a bit awry, perhaps it was actually the Ishi Giant. I doubt that though, since he claimed to have gone back to Kennedy Meadow to get a rope, meaning he had some idea where he was. The area in which he places the tree has been well traversed and heavily logged of sequoias, yet no other account of this tree is known to me. Certainly a big one may lurk in this area. Willard's find of the Ishi Giant proves this. Parts of this area are seldom visited.

A fallen sequoia provides another perspective on the massive volume of a Big Tree.
Photograph by Dick Burns.

The Washington Tree.

Chapter 4:
THE KAWEAH RIVER GROVES

Most of the sequoia groves in this watershed have not been logged. Some trees were cut in the Redwood Mountain Grove from 1873 to 1877, and about one-fourth of the trees were cut in the Atwell Mill area from 1879 to 1920. The Case Mountain Grove has been heavily logged for sequoias, as have several other small areas.

Redwood Mountain Grove

This grove of approximately 4,500 acres, is the largest, with more sequoias than any other. As far as I have been able to determine, it does not have any trees that rival the largest specimens in Giant Forest. It does have two trees that exceed 30,000 cubic feet. The grove covers about 1,907 acres in Kings Canyon National Park, about 500 acres on Giant Sequoia National Monument land, Whittaker Forest, owned by the University of California, and a few trees on private land. Two loop trails through the grove may be reached via a dirt road leading southward from the Quail Flat area on the Generals Highway.

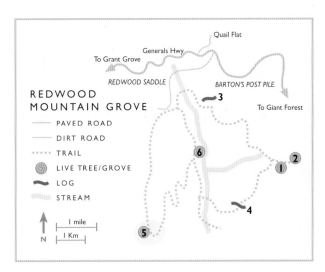

1. Hart 2. Roosevelt 3. Barton's Post Pile 4. Fallen Goliath 5. Sugar Bowl 6. Tall Tree

Hart Tree (#1 RM)

Michael Hart and his son, William H. Hart, discovered the Hart Tree around 1880.[1] The 3.8 mile trail to this tree starts at Redwood Saddle. This forest trail is worth the effort even if the Hart were not there.

Many publications call this the fourth largest tree in the world, but this claim is not true. It was the fourth largest tree measured by the Jourdan Team. It is somewhat of a mystery why this tree was chosen to be measured, but I suspect that the Redwood Mountain Grove needed a champion. In 1931, this grove was in private hands and there was an interest in having this very large grove placed in the national park system. An obviously false set of measurements came to the attention of the Secretary of the Interior, Harold Ickes. It was claimed that this tree was three times the size of the General Sherman Tree. There was another problem. Somebody noticed that a tree just uphill from the Hart was more impressive. The trail was diverted to go by this tree, and a sign indicated that this upper tree was the Hart Tree.[2] I wrote the Hart family and was assured that the lower tree was indeed the real Hart. All photographs I can find confirm this. This is certainly the tree that the Jourdan Team measured in 1931.

The real Hart Tree is impressive. It has a large basal buttress and an extensive burn. It is quite massive above 180 feet. It is a fairly large tree, but no competitor for the really big ones. Mike and I measured it in 1978.

Hart Tree dimensions:		
	ENGLISH	METRIC
HEIGHT	277.9 feet	84.70 meters
GROUND PERIMETER	75.3	22.95
DIAMETER:AT BREAST HIGH	21.3	6.49
AT 60 FEET/18.3 M	14.4	4.39
AT 120 FEET/36.6 M	12.9	3.93
AT 180 FEET/54.9 M	11.3	3.44
VOLUME IGNORING BURNS	34,407 cubic feet	974 cubic meters

Unnamed Tree (Roosevelt or False Hart Tree) (#2 RM)

N. E. Beckwith of the Jourdan Team mentioned this tree seemed larger than the Hart, but said that it was too brushy around it to measure. The lower half of the trunk is more massive, but the tree is shorter with a less massive top. When I first visited these two trees, there were signs on each. The lower sign read "Hart" and the upper tree had "Roosevelt."

Roosevelt Tree dimensions:		
	ENGLISH	METRIC
HEIGHT	260.0 feet	79.24 meters
GROUND PERIMETER	80.0	24.38
DIAMETER:AT BREAST HIGH	22.2	6.77
AT 60 FEET/18.3 M	15.3	4.66
AT 120 FEET/36.6 M	13.9	4.24
AT 180 FEET/54.9 M	9.4	2.86
VOLUME IGNORING BURNS	35,013 cubic feet	991 cubic meters

Mike Law and I measured this tree in 1978 on the same day we measured the Hart. I recall that it was in early winter, and the massive old transit we borrowed from the park became heavier the farther we walked. After our measuring expedition, Mike and I went to dinner at a restaurant near Grant Grove. He ate two successive dinners and half of mine – not at all unusual for him.

Other Things to See in the Redwood Mountain Grove

Barton's Post Pile (#3 RM)

A number of sequoias were cut in this area to make stakes and shakes. This hollow sequoia log served as a cabin, similar to Tharp's Log.

Fallen Goliath   (#4 RM)

This huge hollow log is on a trail southward then westward from the Hart Tree.

Sugar Bowl (#5 RM)

A trail from the Redwood Saddle parking area leads to this fine group of medium sized sequoias on top of Redwood Mountain.

Tall Tree (# 6 RM)

At 307 feet, this is one of the tallest sequoias, as determined by Michael Taylor in 1998. My first edition of this book (1987) refers to two 310-foot sequoias in Redwood Mountain and South Calaveras groves. This information was based on older data. New measurements indicate they are less than 300 feet tall. Some publications refer to a 311-foot tree in the Hazelwood area of Giant Forest. This measurement is based on an older survey and may not be reliable. The tallest, well-measured sequoia, also in the Redwood Mountain Grove, is 311.4 feet tall as measured by Michael Taylor and Chris Atkins in 2001.

Muir and Lost Groves

The Muir Grove covers about 214 acres. It can be reached by a 2.5 mile trail that starts at the west edge of Sequoia National Park's Dorst Campground. Upon entering the grove, you will find an impressive stub of a tree. Although the tree is alive and healthy, too much of its

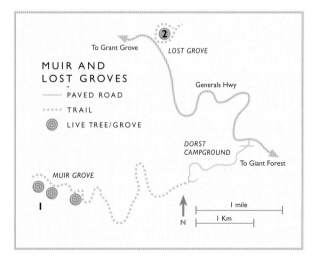

1. Dalton Tree 2. Lost Grove

top is gone for it to be a contender. Near the center of the grove is a tree, which may be the forgotten Dalton Tree (#1 ML), or perhaps the Dalton is a tree with a bigger base to the west. In 1980, two friends, Keith Hindergardt and Ed Kreyenhagen, and I went into the grove with a tape and a crude device for measuring angles. The Dalton had a base perimeter of 74.9 feet and a "good guess" height of 273 feet. The trunk had little taper. It is possible that this tree, despite its small base, could exceed 30,000 cubic feet. In 1997, Jerry Latham and I went to the Muir Grove to have another look at this tree. A controlled burn had wiped out the trail so we never found what I call the Dalton Tree.

The Lost Grove (#2 ML)

Just south of the north entry of Sequoia National Park on the Generals Highway is the small Lost Grove. Its point of interest is a tree with a large, flaring base that is 104.6 feet around at ground level. This tree tapers too much to be a really big one.

Giant Forest

Giant Forest in Sequoia National Park is the most magnificent of all sequoia groves. It features beautiful meadows, the largest trees, and views of the high country from atop the great Moro Rock monolith rising from the grove's southwest edge. Here we find the General Sherman - the largest of all; the Washington – the second or third largest depending on how the volume is calculated; the President – the fourth largest; the Lincoln – the fifth largest; an unnamed tree (unofficially the "Franklin") – the ninth largest; as well as other giants that would be famous were they not in Giant Forest.

Giant Forest, with over 40 miles of trails, is the most accessible of the large groves, covering about 1,880 acres. Highway 198 from Visalia enters Sequoia National Park where it becomes the Generals Highway leading to Giant Forest. From Fresno, Highway 180 enters Kings Canyon National Park and connects to the Generals Highway

General Sherman Tree (#1 GF)

In 1879, cattleman James Wolverton came upon this mighty tree, which he named the General Sherman after the Civil War general. It was renamed the Karl Marx by the people of the Kaweah Colony, who from 1885 to 1890 claimed ownership of Giant Forest for their socialist experiment.[3] The name General Sherman was restored when the area was included in Sequoia National Park.

Not until 1931 did the General Sherman become established as the biggest tree in the world. Before that, there were no rules for comparing large trees. The peak of interest and rivalry over

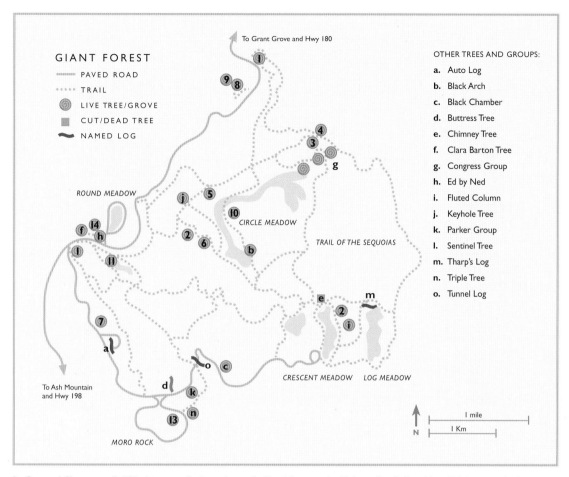

GIANT FOREST

PAVED ROAD
TRAIL
LIVE TREE/GROVE
CUT/DEAD TREE
NAMED LOG

To Grant Grove and Hwy 180

ROUND MEADOW

CIRCLE MEADOW

TRAIL OF THE SEQUOIAS

To Ash Mountain
and Hwy 198

CRESCENT MEADOW   LOG MEADOW

MORO ROCK

OTHER TREES AND GROUPS:

a. Auto Log
b. Black Arch
c. Black Chamber
d. Buttress Tree
e. Chimney Tree
f. Clara Barton Tree
g. Congress Group
h. Ed by Ned
i. Fluted Column
j. Keyhole Tree
k. Parker Group
l. Sentinel Tree
m. Tharp's Log
n. Triple Tree
o. Tunnel Log

1 mile

1 Km

N

1. General Sherman 2. Washington 3. President 4. Chief Sequoyah 5. Lincoln 6. Franklin 7. Monroe 8. General Pershing 9. Column Tree 10. Adams 11. Hazelwood 12. Cleveland 13. NTT 14. Near Ed by Ned

which county had the biggest tree – specifically Fresno or Tulare County – came in the late 1920s when the Jourdan Team was engaged to determine which tree was the largest. The Team's 1931 proclamation that the General Sherman was the largest has remained valid. Mike Law and I measured the Sherman in 1980 and concluded that it was indeed the largest.

The top of the Sherman is a dead limb that at one time served as a new leader. The spike-top condition is normal for older sequoias and is, in most cases, due to basal burns that have cut off the flow of sap to the top. Crown fires can also cause a dead snag top. These same fires clear the ground so that new sequoias can germinate and grow. A large limb, 4 feet in diameter and about 130 feet long, fell from this tree a few years ago. It is just southeast of the tree. The largest limb is almost 7 feet in diameter.

There are taller trees than the General Sherman, and trees with larger bases, but what makes

Measuring the General Sherman. Photograph by Dick Burns.

this tree the champion is its great trunk diameter from breast height to the uppermost big limb. Mike Law and I have searched for larger trees for many years, and we have changed the order in the list of big ones, but the Sherman remains the champion of all living trees.

General Sherman Tree dimensions (1980):		
	ENGLISH	METRIC
HEIGHT	274.9 feet	83.79 meters
GROUND PERIMETER	102.6	31.27
DIAMETER: AT BREAST HIGH	25.1	7.65
AT 60 FEET/18.3 M	17.8	5.43
AT 120 FEET/36.6 M	17.3	5.27
AT 180 FEET/54.9 M	13.7	4.18
VOLUME IGNORING BURNS	52,508 cubic feet	1,487 cubic meters

The General Sherman,
the largest living tree on the earth.

Washington Tree (#2 GF)

This tree is easily reached from the General Sherman parking lot. Take the Alta Trail southward past the Lincoln Tree to a trail leading to Circle Meadow. There is a short side trail to the south that leads to the Washington.

This tree is unusual in many ways. It was known as the Washington Tree as early as 1905, but who named it is not known. How it was missed as a serious contender to the General Sherman is also a question. The tree has a badly damaged and grotesque top about 200 feet up and a new leader has grown past the damage. Earlier observers may have thought that the damage was much lower. One publication says it was 100 feet.

The tree has two tops. The south top is a mere shell and the north leader seems to be an extension of a limb that started far down on the trunk and fused with the trunk. The lower trunk is richly colored and has deeply fluted bark. A large limb on the west side is about 120 feet up. This limb grows horizontally then turns abruptly upward to form a tree in its own right.

This brings up a big question. In the previous edition of this book, I rated the Washington as the second largest sequoia. This is still true if the trunk volume, ignoring losses due to burns, is the criterion used. If the General Grant and the Washington were compared by using their present volume, they would be in a dead heat! Before the crown fire that wrecked the top of the Washington, it could have been the biggest of all!

I made some measurements of this tree as early as 1950, then Mike Law and I measured it in 1976 and 1978. Mike and I get along pretty well most of the time. When we were measuring the Washington, Mike pulled up a crucial marking pin. Without knowing the exact location of the pin, I could no longer make sense of the measurements I had been taking all morning. I recall jumping up and down and screaming. Mike calmed me down by pointing out that I had told him to pull the pin . . . and that he was bigger and stronger than I was.

Washington Tree dimensions:		
	ENGLISH	METRIC
HEIGHT	254.7 feet	77.63 meters
GROUND PERIMETER	101.1	30.81
DIAMETER: AT BREAST HIGH	26.0	7.92
AT 60 FEET/18.3 M	16.6	5.06
AT 120 FEET/36.6 M	16.3	4.97
AT 180 FEET/54.9 M	13.9	4.24
VOLUME IGNORING BURNS	47,850 cubic feet	1,355 cubic meters

President Tree (#3 GF)

From the General Sherman, if the loop is taken clockwise, the Congress Trail leads past the Chief Sequoyah Tree to the President. Named for President Warren G. Harding in 1923, it soon became known as the President Tree.[4] This is the fourth largest measured tree.

Mr. N. E. Beckwith of the Jourdan Team measured this tree around 1932, and thought it was third in size after the Sherman and the Lincoln. At first glance the President doesn't seem special. But when one looks up high on the trunk, what a sight! There are many huge limbs, one about 8 feet in diameter. A compact automobile could be sitting on top of this limb and not be seen! These limbs and the pronounced limb buttress beneath them made measuring this tree a real problem. As we measured upward, the trunk seemed like it was increasing in diameter. At a height of 122 feet, it measured 19.5 feet in diameter. This is not a true measurement of the trunk. The extra width is due to a narrow but long buttress supporting a large limb. The setting for this tree is spectacular. Mike and I measured the President in 1977.

President Tree dimensions:		
	ENGLISH	METRIC
HEIGHT	240.9 feet	73.42 meters
GROUND PERIMETER	93.0	28.35
DIAMETER: AT BREAST HIGH	23.1	7.04
AT 60 FEET/18.3 M	16.8	5.12
AT 120 FEET/36.6 M	16.2	4.94
AT 180 FEET/54.9 M	11.5	3.51
VOLUME IGNORING BURNS	45,148 cubic feet	1,278 cubic meters

Chief Sequoyah Tree (#4 GF)

Just uphill from the President Tree is the massive and very impressive Chief Sequoyah. I think you should sit for a while on the bench near the President and savor the view. There is none better among the sequoias.

The Chief Sequoyah is one of the most startlingly rugged trees in the forest. Park Superintendent John White named it in 1926. Sequoyah was half Cherokee, half German, born about 1770, and known for inventing a syllabary for the Cherokee Nation that allowed them to publish and read in their own tongue.

As is common among giant sequoias, the top is a great, dead snag. Many limbs are stubbed off and broken. The remains of one lies on the ground in front of the tree. The base is fire-

Jerry Latham at the Chief Sequoyah.

scarred. The tree gives the impression of being very old. But size is not a good way to judge the age of a sequoia. For example, increment borings indicate that the General Sherman could possibly be less than 2,150 years old!

Although I made some earlier measurements, Mike and I measured the tree again in 1977. There was one interesting change. The ground perimeter had increased by a foot in about ten years, yet it had not grown that much. People walking around it had exposed more of the root system. It seems to me that people climbing on it to get their pictures taken are abusing this tree – its bark is wearing thin in places.

Chief Sequoyah dimensions:		
	ENGLISH	METRIC
HEIGHT	228.2 feet	69.55 meters
GROUND PERIMETER	90.4	27.55
DIAMETER: AT BREAST HIGH	20.7	6.31
AT 60 FEET/18.3 M	14.6	4.45
AT 120 FEET/36.6 M	14.7	4.48
AT 180 FEET/54.9 M	8.2	2.50
VOLUME IGNORING BURNS	33,608 cubic feet	952 cubic meters

Lincoln Tree (#5 GF)

This old monster of a tree is on the Alta Trail about one mile from the General Sherman. It is the fifth largest tree I have measured. After the Jourdan Team measured the four big ones in 1931, a member of the team, N. E. Beckwith, dissented. He then measured the President and Lincoln trees. He thought that the Lincoln was larger than the Sherman. Colonel White, then park superintendent, is said to have hit the ceiling. In a memorandum to his staff, he told them to keep quiet about it. New provisions for seeing the Sherman had just been completed. He was not about to build another road.

The Lincoln Tree.

I made several attempts to measure the Lincoln in the 1950s and concluded that it was smaller than the Sherman. I have gone over Beckwith's figures, and found why he rated it too high. He did not take enough measurements to see that the trunk did not have a steady taper from top to bottom. He extrapolated too much. At those levels where he actually measured the tree, he and I are in close agreement. Mike and I measured this tree in 1976 and 1980 getting better data than previously obtained.

Lincoln Tree dimensions:		
	ENGLISH	METRIC
HEIGHT	255.8 feet	77.96 meters
GROUND PERIMETER	98.3	29.96
DIAMETER:AT BREAST HIGH	24.5	7.47
AT 60 FEET/18.3 M	16.5	5.03
AT 120 FEET/36.6 M	15.3	4.66
AT 180 FEET/54.9 M	13.3	4.05
VOLUME IGNORING BURNS	44,471 cubic feet	1,259 cubic meters

Unnamed Tree (NWash Tree or Franklin) (#6 GF)

Heading east on the trail leading to the Washington takes one just north of this unnamed tree, which I call the Franklin Tree after Benjamin Franklin, one of our wisest founding fathers. It is the ninth largest tree measured, so I cannot understand why it has been apparently ignored. I can find no histo-

ry of it, yet it has been on a trail for a long time and is located near the well-known Washington.

The Franklin has a huge burn, a thick trunk, and a stubby dead snag top. When I first saw this tree in the early 1950s, the foliage at the top was sparse. It is now filled in, hiding the dead fingers of limbs that reach upward. There is an impressive view of this tree from the top of the ridge just to the east and a few paces north of the trail. This tree illustrates how it is possible that big ones can be overlooked. Mike and I measured this tree several times, the last time in 1980. Some of the earlier measurements were made with questionable instruments.

Franklin dimensions:		
	ENGLISH	METRIC
HEIGHT	223.8 feet	68.21 meters
GROUND PERIMETER	94.8	28.89
DIAMETER:AT BREAST HIGH	21.9	6.67
AT 60 FEET/18.3 M	17.3	5.27
AT 120 FEET/36.6 M	15.1	4.60
AT 180 FEET/54.9 M	12.9	3.93
VOLUME IGNORING BURNS	41,280 cubic feet	1,169 cubic meters

Unnamed Tree (NALog or Monroe) (#7 GF)

Along the road to Moro Rock is another very large tree that seems to have gone unnoticed. This tree is about 200 yards north of the Auto Log, and a short distance east of the road. Perhaps millions of people have driven by it, but few have paid it any attention. I refer to this tree as the NALog tree for Near Auto Log. It is the eleventh largest tree I have located. The tree has dull bark and no distinguishing features except for its great size and massive top. I first noticed this tree in 1950 and made some crude measurements. Mike and I measured it in 1980.

Monroe Tree dimensions:		
	ENGLISH	METRIC
HEIGHT	247.8 feet	75.53 meters
GROUND PERIMETER	91.3	27.83
DIAMETER:AT BREAST HIGH	23.4	7.13
AT 60 FEET/18.3 M	15.9	4.85
AT 120 FEET/36.6 M	14.7	4.48
AT 180 FEET/54.9 M	12.5	3.81
VOLUME IGNORING BURNS	40,104 cubic feet	1,135 cubic meters

The Ben Franklin Tree.
Dwight Willard (left) with Wendell Flint.

The Monroe Tree. Mark Tilchen (left) accompanies Don Holloway on his first visit to the giant sequoias.

General Pershing (#8 GF)

Former Park Superintendent Colonel White named this tree in 1926 for the commander of the American Expeditionary Force in World War I.[5] You can find it by taking the trail that starts on the road south of the General Sherman. After a short hike of perhaps 300 yards, the remnant of an old trail cuts back north and downhill to the Pershing. The lower trunk is massive and the top is a tapering dead snag. It is very impressive and worth viewing. Mike Law, Jerry Latham, Bill Croft, and I measured this tree in 1991.

Pershing dimensions:		
	ENGLISH	METRIC
HEIGHT	246.0 feet	74.98 meters
GROUND PERIMETER	91.2	27.80
DIAMETER:AT BREAST HIGH	21.5	6.55
AT 60 FEET/18.3 M	15.2	4.63
AT 120 FEET/36.6 M	12.3	3.75
AT 180 FEET/54.9 M	11.9	3.63
VOLUME IGNORING BURNS	35,855 cubic feet	1,015 cubic meters

Unnamed Tree (Npersh or Column Tree) (#9 GF)

About one hundred yards west and slightly north of the Pershing is another large sequoia. Traveling southward from the Pershing, it is visible downhill from the trail. I refer to this tree as the NPersh (Near Pershing Tree). Mike and I like to call this the Column Tree because of its shape. The massive top and lack of taper in the trunk is what gives this tree its size.

I spotted this tree in the 1950s, but did not measure it. Mike Law brought it to my attention, pointing out that it looked big to him. Mike, Jerry Latham, David Latham, and I measured it in the fall of 1995. Unfortunately, there were a few spots of hot coals remaining from a controlled burn, so one transit line was not finished. Mike and I finished the job in 1998.

Column Tree dimensions:		
	ENGLISH	METRIC
HEIGHT	243.8 feet	74.31 meters
GROUND PERIMETER	93.0	28.35
DIAMETER:AT BREAST HIGH	23.3	7.10
AT 60 FEET/18.3 M	14.9	4.54
AT 120 FEET/36.6 M	13.7	4.18
AT 180 FEET/54.9 M	12.5	3.81
VOLUME IGNORING BURNS	37,295 cubic feet	1,056 cubic meters

Unnamed Tree (NCC – Near Cattle Cabin Tree or Adams Tree) (#10 GF)

Although this tree is not on a trail, it is easy to find. From the General Sherman, take the trail to the Cattle Cabin. Continuing from the cabin towards Crescent Meadow, you will come to an opening in the forest. The tree is to the east, several hundred yards away.

There was a problem getting good measurements on this tree. From about 90 feet up, the trunk is very irregular with many limb buttresses and lots of foliage. The top is a maze of limbs, so I was not sure what I was seeing through the transit telescope. The base is not imposing. I have a feeling that we have the volume somewhat too large. Mike and I measured this tree in

Adams Tree dimensions:		
	ENGLISH	METRIC
HEIGHT	250.6 feet	76.38 meters
GROUND PERIMETER	83.3	25.39
DIAMETER:AT BREAST HIGH	20.5	6.25
AT 60 FEET/18.3 M	16.9	5.15
AT 120 FEET/36.6 M	14.3	4.36
AT 180 FEET/54.9 M	12.1	3.69
VOLUME IGNORING BURNS	38,956 cubic feet	1,103 cubic meters

1989, and then squabbled about it for years. He thought that it was a great big one, and I thought it was smaller. I think I finally won the argument, but Mike is still bigger than I am.

Unnamed Tree (Hazelwood Tree) (#11 GF)

Located on a hillside just west of the Hazelwood Nature Trail, this is an imposing tree, especially when seen from the east. It is unusually tall for a tree of such size. Its base is on a slant, which means the breast height measurement is high. Mike and I measured this tree in 1989, but its measurements are somewhat uncertain because not enough measurements could be made on a second transit line.

COMMENTARY BY MIKE LAW

During my 30 years of searching and measuring large sequoias with Wendell, three trees that we had measured are now victims of lightening strikes and fire. The latest casualty, the Hazelwood Tree, once the 17th largest tree in the world at 36,228 cubic feet, lost half its trunk in late May or early June of 2002 during a lightening storm.

Dr. Robert Van Pelt and I discovered the shattered giant during a trip to Giant Forest in June 2002. This is still a site worth seeing. A huge fire scar climbs the trunk and sequoia wood is strewn about. At the time of our visit, the tree, with some limbs remaining, was still alive.

Cleveland Tree (#12 GF)

John Broder, a concessionaire, named this tree for President Cleveland in 1902.[6] This tree stands near the northeast corner of Crescent Meadow, adjacent to the loop trail. I often have fun with people by telling them to watch for a very large sequoia within a few feet of the trail. Then I walk them right by it without their noticing. I do cheat – when we get close, I call their attention to something in the meadow, such as a deer.

Cleveland Tree dimensions:		
	ENGLISH	METRIC
HEIGHT	250.5 feet	76.35 meters
GROUND PERIMETER	79.8	24.32
DIAMETER:AT BREAST HIGH	22.9	6.98
AT 60 FEET/18.3 M	14.1	4.30
AT 120 FEET/36.6 M	13.8	4.21
AT 180 FEET/54.9 M	12.9	3.93
VOLUME IGNORING BURNS	31,336 cubic feet	887 cubic meters

Mark Tilchen (left) and Mike Law at the Column Tree.

Its trunk tapers very little, but it is not heavy enough to rank high among the super giants. Bob Arp and I measured it in 1980 with a borrowed transit that wasn't very good, so the data are a little questionable. John Muir had visited nearby Tharp's Log, so I have reason to believe he knew of this tree. I think I can see where he may have scraped a band of charcoal off a fire-scarred part of the trunk in order to take a ring count to determine its age.

Unnamed Tree (NTT - Near Triple Tree or Hamilton Tree) (#13 GF)

This tree is a little north of the Triple Tree on the one-way loop road to Moro Rock. It has an irregular trunk, making good measurements a little difficult. Mike and I measured it in 1993.

Dimensions of the Hamilton:		
	ENGLISH	METRIC
HEIGHT	238.5 feet	72.69 meters
GROUND PERIMETER	82.6	25.18
DIAMETER:AT BREAST HIGH	22.0	6.71
AT 60 FEET/18.3 M	15.1	4.60
AT 120 FEET/36.6 M	13.7	4.18
AT 180 FEET/54.9 M	12.7	3.87
VOLUME IGNORING BURNS	32,783 cubic feet	928 cubic meters

Unnamed Tree (NEdByNed or Near Ed by Ned) (#14 GF)

Another tree with an impressive lower trunk is found to the west of the south end of Round Meadow. There is a fallen sequoia above it and it is located just above a large pair of trees called Ed by Ned. Jerry Latham and I measured this tree in 1997. We need to measure it more to be sure of its size, but I don't think the present figures are far off.

NEdByNed Tree dimensions:		
	ENGLISH	METRIC
HEIGHT	250.8 feet	76.44 meters
GROUND PERIMETER	79.4	24.20
DIAMETER:AT BREAST HIGH	19.8	6.03
AT 60 FEET/18.3 M	16.0	4.88
AT 120 FEET/36.6 M	13.1	3.99
AT 180 FEET/54.9 M	5.8	1.77
VOLUME IGNORING BURNS	30,333 cubic feet	859 cubic meters

The Auto Log in the 1920s. Photograph from NPS collection, Sequoia National Park.

Other Large Sequoias and Sights in Giant Forest

There are unmeasured trees in Giant Forest that could top 30,000 cubic feet. One is at the junction of the Alta and Congress trails. Another is in what was once the Giant Forest Lodge area.

Auto Log

Located on the Moro Rock Road, this log fell in 1917.

Black Arch

This tree straddles the trail at the south end of Circle Meadow. This is a fairly large tree named in 1922 by Park Superintendent Colonel John White.

Black Chamber

Located on the north side of the road to Crescent Meadow 400 yards east of the Tunnel Log. This tree is remarkable in that it is mostly a charred shell, but is still alive and healthy.

Buttress Tree

Located east of Trinity Corner, this tree fell in 1959 and is now an imposing log.

Chimney Tree

Found at the north end of Crescent Meadow, this hollow shell of a tree was killed in 1919 by a camper who built a campfire next to its base.

Clara Barton Tree

Found on the trail going from Round Meadow to the Giant Forest Museum – a beautiful specimen.

Congress Group

This group is found on the Congress Trail loop below the President Tree. It consists of two dense stands of giant sequoias – the Senate and the House. This is a must see.

Ed by Ned

This large, but not fully measured pair, is just west of the south end of Round Meadow. They were probably named by Mrs. A. W. Childs in 1906 for John Jordan and Ed Fudge.

Fluted Column

This interesting tree is on the east side of Crescent Meadow, south of the Cleveland Tree. It has an unusual limb structure and a trunk that looks like a Grecian column.

Four Guardsmen

The Generals Highway below the Giant Forest Museum runs through this group. They were named by George Welsh, who surveyed the road.

Keyhole Tree

This wreck of a tree is near the west side of the Alta Trail about 800 yards south of the Lincoln. It is the burnt remnant of a very large tree that is still alive. Judge Walter Fry named it for the large hole in its trunk, which resembles a keyhole.

Parker Group

About 400 yards beyond the Buttress Tree on the east side of Crescent Meadow Road is this fine stand of trees. Named for his family by Captain James Parker, who was charged by the U. S. Army to protect the area in 1893.

Sentinel Tree

This magnificent tree is located on the Generals Highway in front of the Giant Forest Museum. It is the first really big sequoia seen when entering the grove from the south. The Sentinel is 257.6 feet tall, has a mean base diameter of 28.3 feet, and is 11.4 feet in diameter at 90 feet above the ground.

Tharp's Log

This log is found at the north end of Log Meadow. Cattleman Hale Tharp found it in 1858 after being shown the Giant Forest area by some friendly Potwisha Indians. He lived in it from time to time. James Wolverton, another cattleman, lived in the log for a few summers. John Muir visited Tharp in this log in 1875. The living quarters are about 54.5 feet long and 4 to 8 feet high.

Tunnel Log. Photo by Katie O'Hara-Kelly, Sequoia National Park collection.

Triple Tree

Located on the east side of the one-way Moro Rock loop road, this is actually three trees whose bases have fused.

Tunnel Log

This tree, which fell in 1937, is now a drive-through log across the Crescent Meadow Road.

Atwell Mill-East Fork Groves

This magnificent complex of groves in the East Fork of the Kaweah watershed area is reached via the Mineral King Road, which branches off Highway 198 below the south entrance to Sequoia National Park. The road is mostly hard surface, but steep and winding. The complex occupies an area of about 2,300 acres.

The largest area is the Atwell Mill lobe, north of the river. The second largest, the East Fork lobe, is mostly south of the river and is tenuously connected to the Atwell Mill lobe. A slightly detached unit called the Redwood Creek Grove is just to the west of the Atwell Mill lobe. A

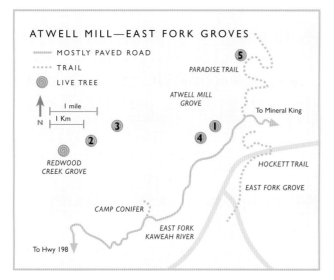

ATWELL MILL—EAST FORK GROVES

——— MOSTLY PAVED ROAD

········· TRAIL

◎ LIVE TREE

N

| 1 mile
| 1 Km

PARADISE TRAIL

ATWELL MILL GROVE

To Mineral King

REDWOOD CREEK GROVE

HOCKETT TRAIL

EAST FORK GROVE

CAMP CONIFER

EAST FORK KAWEAH RIVER

To Hwy 198

1. Dean **2.** Diamond **3.** AD **4.** Arm **5.** Tunnel

second detached unit is east of the East Fork lobe. About one-fourth of the Atwell Mill lobe has been logged of giant sequoias, but many untouched areas are left. There are three trees of great size in the Atwell Mill area.

Dean Tree (#1 AE)

Mrs. Grace Alles, whose father was a logger in this grove around 1900, told me of the existence of the Dean Tree. When I first looked for this tree in 1950, the name 'Dean' was carved in a charred area on the trunk. I could no longer make out the name in 1983. The name was in honor of an early pioneer, but I can find no record of this tree in the Sequoia National Park files.

There is no trail to this tree. It can be found by taking an abandoned road to a now destroyed cabin. This old road leads uphill from a point west of the Alles Cabin site. From the cabin site, follow the watershed just east of the cabin site upstream to some boulders, and then go over the ridge westward to the tree. It is a good looking tree but tapers too much to be a really big one.

Mike and I had gone to the tree to take pictures and find transit points. The next day we set out to do our measurements. On the way, we stopped at an old cabin site on private land. Two rangers swooped in on us and wanted to know why we were at this site. I told them that I knew the owner, which was true. I also said that we had a really big tree to measure. One ranger said that he had been in this area for years and that he knew of no big one. I invited the rangers to tag along. Mike and I measured this tree in 1973.

Dean Tree dimensions:		
	ENGLISH	METRIC
HEIGHT	235.8 feet	71.87 meters
GROUND PERIMETER	96.3	29.35
DIAMETER: AT BREAST HIGH	20.3	6.19
AT 60 FEET/18.3 M	14.6	4.45
AT 120 FEET/36.6 M	13.6	4.15
AT 180 FEET/54.9 M	8.9	2.71
VOLUME IGNORING BURNS	32,333 cubic feet	915 cubic meters

Unnamed Tree (Diamond Tree) (#2 AE)

I call this the Diamond Tree because of a peculiar diamond shaped scar high up on the trunk. The tree appears to be very big from the south, but much smaller when seen from up a nearby stream. It is on what was once a trail from Camp Conifer to Oriole Lake. This unmaintained trail will be difficult to follow. It starts from the abandoned road that leads to Camp Conifer, at a gated road approximately two miles west on the Mineral King road. The Diamond Tree can be found by going to the northwest corner of the meadow-like area in Camp Conifer, then following the west edge of the grove until the drainage into the Redwood Creek area is reached. Here the old trail turns westward to the Redwood Creek unit. The tree is in the switchback of the trail.

This tree is on a steep slope. The base extends downward toward the creek. The breast high measurement put the tape maybe 16 feet above the ground on the downhill side, whereas it is just 4.5 feet above the high point of ground. It is a relatively tall tree with a much flattened trunk. It appears much thinner when seen from up the creek than from across the creek. Mike Law, Dennis Coggins, and I started measuring this tree in 1983. A year later Mike and I, along with some friends, finished the job.

	Diamond Tree dimensions:	
	ENGLISH	METRIC
HEIGHT	286.0 feet	87.17 meters
GROUND PERIMETER	95.3	29.05
DIAMETER:AT BREAST HIGH	18.4	5.61
AT 60 FEET/18.3 M	15.1	4.60
AT 120 FEET/36.6 M	13.8	4.21
AT 180 FEET/54.9 M	7.0	2.13
VOLUME IGNORING BURNS	35,292 cubic feet	999 cubic meters

Unnamed Tree (AD Tree) (#3 AE)

This tree I call the AD Tree for Above Diamond Tree. It can be reached by going to the Diamond Tree, then heading upstream a short distance, crossing over to the next drainage to the right, then proceeding to just below the top of the ridge. The tree is at the south end of a clear space in the forest. The drainage to the south of the one that goes past the Diamond is not well defined, so it may take a little time to find the correct way to the tree.

Like the Diamond Tree, it is on a slope, such that the breast height measurement is high on the trunk on the downhill side, making the diameter at this height smaller than might be

expected. The main trunk is quite thick, and together with its modest height, gives the impression of great size. Mike Law, Jerry Latham, and I measured this tree in 1986.

AD Tree dimensions:		
	ENGLISH	METRIC
HEIGHT	242.4 feet	73.88 meters
GROUND PERIMETER	99.0	30.17
DIAMETER:AT BREAST HIGH	17.8	5.43
AT 60 FEET/18.3 M	15.2	4.63
AT 120 FEET/36.6 M	13.5	4.11
AT 180 FEET/54.9 M	11.7	3.57
VOLUME IGNORING BURNS	34,706 cubic feet	983 cubic meters

Other Notable Trees in the Atwell Mill Area

Arm Tree (#4 AE)

This unusual tree is on an unmaintained and now obliterated trail near the top of the ridge east of Camp Conifer. It seems to have the largest limb of any tree in the world – 12 feet in diameter! The trunk up to the limb, which is about 40 feet up, is massive. Above the limb, the tree splits into four leaders.

The Arm Tree – the world's largest known tree limb.

Just below this tree is a pair of trees that figured into a mystery during the logging days of this region. Lady Alles, who lived in a nearby cabin, told me that from time to time a strange "whoomping" sound reverberated through the forest. One day, around 1975, my cousin Robert Bergen and I were walking the Paradise Trail when we heard this whoomping sound. We started cross country toward the sound and discovered the big limb tree, which I called the Arm Tree. The sound was coming from the pair of trees below the Arm Tree. Fire had hollowed out their trunks, which were rubbing together high up, acting as resonators and producing the sound.

Tunnel Tree (#5 AE)

This tree is at the head of a meadow, just west of the Paradise Trail at the top of the grove, about three miles from the trailhead. Its huge flared base has been burned all the way through

The AD Tree.

and three compact cars could be driven abreast halfway through it. The tree is a remarkable 57 feet across its vast base. Cracks are appearing in the remaining trunk.

South Fork of the Kaweah

South of the town of Three Rivers is a country road – the South Fork, which leads to a campground just inside the Sequoia National Park boundary. Two maintained trails start in this area. On the south side of the river is a trail to the Garfield area. It is a tiring hike if you want to look around and get back to the campground in one day, but it can be done. The grove, which is made up of the Garfield and Dillonwood areas, lies within two different watersheds. Though most grove lists show Garfield and Dillonwood as separate groves, this is not the case. It is one big grove covering approximately 2,330 acres in the national park and 572 acres in the national monument.

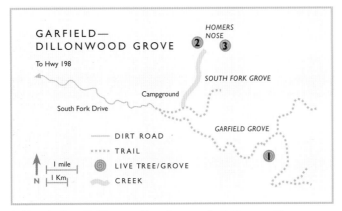

1. King Arthur 2. Phantom Tree (rumored) 3. Phantom Tree

Unnamed Tree in the Garfield Area (King Arthur) (#1 GD)
I refer to this tree as the King Arthur even though the park does not recognize that name. I call it that for the legendary king who was noted for pulling swords out of rocks. The tree is found by walking the main trail about halfway through the grove to where a small stream cuts across the trail, and the trail itself changes direction and goes to the northeast corner of the grove. From the trail walk uphill, paralleling the small stream just to its west. The tree is close to this watershed. Two large trees stand above it.

  Back around 1949, when I was just getting interested in hunting for large sequoias, a ranger said that a hiker coming up from the Dillonwood area had crossed over a ridge and spotted a tree of great dimensions. He had made an attempt to get to it, but lost his view of it and could not relocate it. There were similar tales about a "Phantom Tree" that was supposed to be in the Homer's Nose Grove, which lies to the north on the other side of the river. I'll have more to say about the Phantom later.

  By 1977, the Garfield area had been inventoried, and several large trees were shown on the inventory map. In the fall of 1978, two fellow tree hunters, Bob Walker and Gus Boik, went

The King Arthur Tree.
Dennis Coggins in foreground.

with me to look for these trees. I spotted the largest one I could see and called Bob over to help me make a few measurements. Later my cousin Robert Bergen and I made a few more measurements. However, it was not until 1985 that we were finally able to make some transit measurements. Mike Law and I gathered most of the data, with Jerry helping out. The other members of the party were too pooped to do anything. I had to depend on poor instrumentation for one line and we needed two transit lines to really nail this tree down, but time ran out. As it was, three of us got back to the campground after dark. Mike's knee was hurting, Robert's legs were cramping, and so were mine. Jerry and friends had flitted on down ahead of us, and they had the flashlight! When we did not arrive as expected, they called the ranger. He told them not to worry; if he knew me I would probably wobble out sooner or later. King Arthur needs more work done on it. It could be larger or smaller than I now calculate it to be.

This tree embodies many of the characteristics of the "lost biggest one." For the first 60 feet it is nearly equal to the General Sherman and just slightly shorter than the Sherman. It is on fairly steep ground, so the breast high diameter is higher than on the Sherman. About two years ago, a friend, Ed Carley, visited the tree and said that it was now possible to get a tape all the way around it on the ground. I could not do this previously because of a log rolled up against the tree.

King Arthur dimensions:		
	ENGLISH	METRIC
HEIGHT	270.3 feet	82.38 m
GROUND PERIMETER	104.2	31.76
DIAMETER:AT BREAST HIGH	23.1	7.04
AT 60 FEET/18.3 M	15.6	4.75
AT 120 FEET/36.6 M	14.3	4.36
AT 180 FEET/54.9 M	11.2	3.41
VOLUME IGNORING BURNS	40,656 cubic feet	1,151 cubic meters

Does the Kaweah Hold a Tree Exceeding the Sherman?

Frankly, I'd say the probability is low. Most of this area has been inventoried and mapped to show the location of every sequoia of any size. All of the groves within the national parks have been carefully mapped. There are several small acreages of sequoias outside of the national parks, but none of them contain really Big Trees. The largest I know of is a tree in the Case Mountain Grove on Bureau of Land Management land. It has a breast high diameter of about 17 feet. In 1966, Richard Burns representing the Park Service, and Thomas Harvey and Richard

Hartesveldt from San Jose State University, looked for the big one rumored to be in the grove.

From time to time, I hear a rumor that a tree larger than the General Sherman is hiding in Giant Forest. I have seen most of this grove, and I have concluded that this rumored tree may be the Lincoln Tree because of Mr. Beckwith's claim. Another possibility is now a great dead snag east of the NCC Tree. When I first saw it, there was bark on it. Now it is somewhat reduced by fire. A team from the University of Arizona estimated its age as 3,000 years.

The Phantom Tree Rumors

There is a persistent rumor about a "Phantom Tree" under Homer's Nose (#2 GD). The story, which started in a newspaper article, stated that Fred W. Clough, an engineer, said he found a great tree about a mile east of Homer's Nose (an imposing monolith), that was 44 rifle lengths around as measured by Wesley Warren, who was with him.[7] The rifle length was given as four feet long, which would make the tree 176 feet around! And that was supposedly 7 feet above the ground! No other giant sequoia comes close to this size. Sometime before 1934, Ernest Dudly reported that he had found the tree and that it was 150 to 160 feet around. This tree is described as being in a basin surrounded by huge rocks. The top was reported as being broken off, but it was still fairly tall. According to E. T. Scoyen, Sequoia National Park superintendent in the 1950s, searches by Weldon F. Heald of the Sierra Club failed to find the tree. However, in a letter to me, Mr. Scoyen said that a Sierra Club expedition had found the tree, and that it was much smaller than the Sherman.

In a letter from Frank L. Kenwood to Bob Walker, who had become an enthusiastic hunter of the Phantom Tree, Mrs. Geyel Brooks, the wife of a district ranger and a great niece of Mr. Clough, had found the tree and had measured it with a lariat. These measurements are not known, and since Mr. and Mrs. Brooks are deceased, there is little chance of recovering this information. I have heard from an unknown source that the tree is about 101 feet around on the ground.

Bob Walker, Ros Rioux, and I looked for the tree in the grove just east of the Homer's Nose Grove in 1980. We didn't find it. We also tried to reach the Homer's Nose Grove Tree. We got to within a mile of it, then had to give up because one of my legs stopped working.

In 1982, fisherman Robert Schweizer reported to the resident ranger in the South Fork Campground that he saw a huge tree in the Cahoon Creek Grove, which is northeast of Homer's Nose. The next year, Ranger Tom Jeffrey, Bob Walker, Ros Rioux, and Gus Boik checked the story out. No great tree was found. I later talked to Mr. Schweizer who had been back to the grove. He is pretty sure that what he saw was two trees close together.

Mr. Schweizer met with me at my home and decided to take a side trip on his next fishing expedition to the Homer's Nose Grove to find what was inventoried as the largest tree in that grove. He and his fishing companions found it. It was clearly the largest tree they had seen in the grove (#2 GD). It had a broken top and little taper. A topographical map of the area showed it to be in a basin of sorts. But there was one enormous problem – the tape! It only had a ground perimeter of 76.7 feet! The tree was on such steep ground that a breast high perimeter was too difficult to take. They did get a measurement at 3.5 feet. Here it measured 62 feet around. The rifle first used to measure Clough's monster tree might have been a pop-gun. And whether it was a mile east of Homer's Nose was a problem. It was right against the base of the monolith, maybe a mile from its top.

Later (in 1994, I think), Bob Walker went back to the Board Camp Grove, just east of the Homer's Nose Grove. The park inventory showed a tree (#3 GD) of the same size as the tree in the Homer's Nose Grove – and it had a broken top. Bob found it. The tree overlooked a steep ravine and had an enormous flange of bark running down the slope. It was impossible to walk around. Bob said it might afford a perimeter of over 150 feet. At breast height, it was a little over 19 feet in diameter. A map check showed it to be about a mile from Homer's Nose. I think that this is the Phantom Tree. It probably looks extremely large from the downhill side.

Schweizer also says that there is a pretty big one in the South Fork Grove. I have looked for it. I did find a very large fallen tree close to the area he described, but it certainly was never a rival. The park inventory shows trees that are at least 20 feet in diameter breast high. There are some in the Redwood Mountain, two in the Redwood Meadow Grove complex, three in the Oriole Grove, one in the Eden Grove, one or two in the East Fork lobe of the Atwell-East Fork Grove complex, and maybe one in the South Fork Grove. I have not seen all of these trees. There are three trees in the Suwanee Grove that exceed 20 feet, and I have seen two of them. They are not giants. According to the inventory, there is a huge 25-foot diameter breast high dead snag in the grove. I have seen most of the inventoried trees of any size. There is one in the Garfield Grove that I have seen from a distance that may be interesting.

Does the Phantom exist? The answer is, probably not. But could be . . . maybe. There are groves in this watershed I have not mentioned. No giants are shown in the inventory of these groves. I have not found any real giants in the sequoia forests outside the parks in this watershed. Mike and I have spotted large sequoias below the trail, but we were always too pooped to investigate. Nearly all the groves in this watershed have been inventoried. This is not true of the parts of the Garfield-Dillonwood Grove that were either private or in the Giant Sequoia National Monument in the Tule River watershed.

Homer's Nose from the Garfield Grove. Rumors of a Phantom Tree, larger than the General Sherman, persist to this day.

Mountain Home State Forest. Photograph by Dick Burns.

Chapter 5:
THE TULE RIVER GROVES

There are a large number of giant sequoias in the Tule River watershed and many areas that have been logged. The large Dillonwood Grove, the northernmost of these groves, is largely cut over for sequoias. The fringes, where most of the remaining sequoias are located, are on Giant Sequoia National Monument land. The Mountain Home Grove regions have been logged extensively, but a large part of the grove has not been logged. Relatively small parts of the Black Mountain Grove have had sequoias cut. Some of the groves in this watershed are very large, namely the Dillonwood lobe of the Garfield-Dillonwood Grove, the Mountain Home Grove, the Black Mountain Grove, and the Belknap Complex (McIntyre Grove).

Dillonwood

The heart of this grove has been cut over for sequoias as late as 1956. It was recently added to Sequoia National Park. There is no easy way to the fringes of the grove, which is on Giant Sequoia National Monument land. The largest tree I have heard of is 20 feet in diameter breast high. The easiest way to get close to the grove is to take Highway 198 to Frazier Valley Road, which runs southward. Then go east on Mountain Home (Balch Park) Road. Then turn north and take Road 19S09 as far as you can. It is possible for a big one to be hiding on Forest Service land.

Mountain Home Grove

This is my second favorite grove after Giant Forest. It has the second largest number of really Big Trees. It is one of the easiest groves to explore on maintained trails and abandoned logging roads. It rivals the Redwood Mountain Grove as the largest grove of all. As I see it, the Middle Tule Grove and the Silver Creek Grove are really units of the Mountain Home Grove. The total size could be over 3,000 acres.

Access to the grove is by one of two roads. Coming from the north, take Highway 198 eastward from Visalia, turn south on Yokohl Valley Road, then east on the Mountain Home Road. There are signs for "Balch Park," a county park within the grove. From the south, take Highway 190 from Porterville to Springville, and then take the road north from the east end of Springville. The

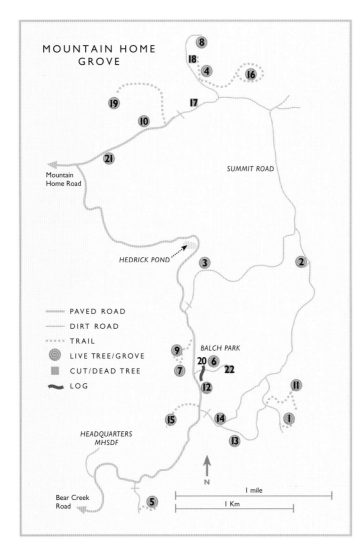

MOUNTAIN HOME
GROVE

SUMMIT ROAD

Mountain
Home Road

HEDRICK POND

PAVED ROAD
DIRT ROAD
TRAIL
LIVE TREE/GROVE
CUT/DEAD TREE
LOG

BALCH PARK

HEADQUARTERS
MHSDF

Bear Creek
Road

N

1 mile
1 Km

1. Genesis 2. Summit Road 3. Euclid 4. Adam 5. Methuselah 6. Allen Russell 7. Three Fingered Jack 8. Five Sisters 9. Harlequin Trees 10. Hercules 11. Great Bonsai 12. Lady Alice 13. Old Jobe 14. Oliver Twist 15. Wishbone 16. Sequoia group 17. Centennial Stump 18. Eve 19. Sequoia group 20. Hollow Log 21. Nero 22. Sawed Tree

first road leading eastward is Bear Creek Road. This leads to Mountain Home and Balch Park.

Genesis Tree (#1 MH)

In July of 1985, Mike and I were driving the back roads of Mountain Home State Forest on the lookout for large sequoias. Mike spotted a great trunk through the trees, and insisted I find a way to drive closer to it. We were able to park a few hundred yards from the tree, and then walk up through tall bracken ferns to the tree. I heard Mike say "Oh, wow!" These were not his actual words, which if used in print would offend some. This tree seemed to rival the famous Boole Tree. Although the base was no match for the Boole, the main trunk seemed to be heavier. A few days later, we returned with David Dulitz, the manager of Mountain Home State Forest, and a transit. Dulitz at first thought that the tree was inferior to the Adam Tree in the same grove, but began to reserve judgment when preliminary measurements indicated that the tree was a really big one.

Dulitz, his staff, and I decided upon the name "Genesis" for this imposing tree in keeping with the biblical and mythological theme of the other named trees in the forest. I find it an appropriate name, with Adam and Eve and Old Methuselah not far away. I suspect that Dulitz was apprehensive about Mike's calling the tree the "Adam Smasher" because it exceeded the Adam Tree, the largest tree in the grove known at the time.

It is not hard to find this tree. First, take the Summit Road just south of Balch Park. On the left, you will come to the Oliver Twist Tree, noted for its spiral pattern of bark. Beyond that the Summit Road turns north; a narrower road proceeds ahead, and a less traveled road goes right. Take the road straight ahead. Pass Old Jobe, the remnants of a true giant on the right. Then the Dogwood Meadow comes into view, with a large leaning tree threatening to fall and a great double tree at the head of the meadow. Go to the three-way junction and keep to the right. Take the road to the sharp right and you'll find a parking space near the end of the road. A trail leads a short distance eastward to the Genesis. Stop at the little museum at Balch Park to see a map to this tree.

Mike and I made several trips to the Genesis in 1985 to take measurements. Measuring the tree presented a problem. A thicket of dogwood obscured the trunk from a very desirable transit line. I asked for permission from the Forest Service to whack the dogwood down, thinking the tree was on their territory. This was approved. We whacked. When Dulitz saw what we had done, he informed us that the tree was in his territory by a few yards. However, he did not frown too much at our chopping. The dogwood has now grown up to obscure the view again, as he said it would.

The Genesis Tree.

Perhaps one reason this tree was not seen for what it is - a true giant - is that the best view of it would be from a thicket of brush. The trail approaches it from the narrow side. We were not the first people to notice the tree. There is graffiti in the burn cavities, now almost unreadable, that indicates that the tree had been noted by Harrison White and Willie Moore about 1887. I checked with the Moore family, who happened to live a block from me, and they verified that a Moore was in the area at that time. Mike and I measured this tree in 1985.

Genesis Tree dimensions:		
	ENGLISH	METRIC
HEIGHT	253.0 feet	77.11 meters
GROUND PERIMETER	85.3	26.00
DIAMETER:AT BREAST HIGH	22.5	6.86
AT 60 FEET/18.3 M	16.9	5.15
AT 120 FEET/36.6 M	15.0	4.57
AT 180 FEET/54.9 M	10.5	3.20
VOLUME IGNORING BURNS	41,897 cubic feet	1,186 cubic meters

Unnamed Tree (Summit Road Tree) (#2 MH)

In the autumn of 1988 Mike, Jerry, and I were returning from a brushy hike up Silver Creek east of Mountain Home to see what was in the Silver Creek Grove. We did not find much of interest in this area. It had been a long day. On our way out, we were going along the Summit Road. I was driving, Jerry was snoring, and Mike was looking.

Almost simultaneously Mike and I spotted a big one near the road that was so obscured by fir trees that we had driven past it many times and failed to see it. Jerry was still out and missed his chance to find a big one. I shall refer to this tree as the Summit Road Tree. It is just west of the Summit Road and about 600 yards from the junction of the Summit Road and a road that leads to Hedrick Pond.

The tree is of medium height, has a relatively small base, a heavy trunk and few burn scars. There is a downed log against the trunk on the south side. This is a good example of how a large tree can be overlooked because its basal diameter is not impressive. Mike and I measured this tree in 1988.

Summit Road Tree dimensions:		
	ENGLISH	METRIC
HEIGHT	244.0 feet	74.37 meters
GROUND PERIMETER	82.2	25.05
DIAMETER:AT BREAST HIGH	20.6	6.28
AT 60 FEET/18.3 M	16.4	5.00
AT 120 FEET/36.6 M	13.6	4.15
AT 180 FEET/54.9 M	10.5	3.20
VOLUME IGNORING BURNS	36,600 cubic feet	1,036 cubic meters

Unnamed Tree (Euclid Tree) (#3 MH)

Bob Walker and I identified this tree in 1989. I like to call it the Euclid Tree after the famous geometry master in keeping with the names of other major trees in this area where classical or biblical names abound. It is found just north of the road that cuts across the forest from a point south of Hedrick Pond to the Summit Road. It is perhaps 400 yards from the Mountain Home Road. It is a relatively tall tree and very imposing from the downhill side. Bob and I measured this tree in 1989.

Mike Law and the Euclid Tree.

Euclid Tree Dimensions:		
	ENGLISH	METRIC
HEIGHT	272.7 feet	83.11 m
GROUND PERIMETER	83.4	25.42
DIAMETER: AT BREAST HIGH	20.3	6.19
AT 60 FEET/18.3 M	15.2	4.63
AT 120 FEET/36.6 M	14.2	4.33
AT 180 FEET/54.9 M	11.9	3.63
VOLUME IGNORING BURNS	36,122 cubic feet	1,023 cubic meters

Adam Tree (#4 MH)

The Adam Tree appears to have been named by Jesse Hoskins around 1884. He was also responsible for the room carved out of the Hercules Tree. The Adam can be reached by using the loop trail starting near Shake Camp, or if you don't mind a bumpy road, it is possible to drive near the tree by taking the road going north from the Enterprise Mill area for about one-quarter of a mile. The loop trail is just to the north of the road. Go west on this trail, cross a small watershed and then go east to the tree.

This is surely one of the most imposing trees in the Mountain Home Grove. The trunk appears very massive from the downhill side. The Adam is nearly a perfect specimen except for a burned area on the uphill side. Its top does not show a visible dead spike, which is unusual for a tree of such size. It has massive limbs reminding one of the President Tree in Giant Forest. The trunk tapers too much above the first big limb for the tree to be one of the very big ones.

Norman Cook, the Mountain Home State Forest manager, and David Dulitz measured this tree in 1978. Mike and I also measured it in 1978. Although we did not know of each other's efforts, our results are very similar. I regard the height obtained by Cook and Dulitz as being the better figure; because the measuring method I used was convenient, but not well suited for the total height. I shall use their figure for the total height in the data given below.

Mike Law at the Adam Tree.

Adam Tree dimensions:		
	ENGLISH	METRIC
HEIGHT	247.4 feet	75.40 meters
GROUND PERIMETER	94.2	28.71
DIAMETER: AT BREAST HIGH	23.0	7.01
AT 60 FEET/18.3 M	16.2	4.94
AT 120 FEET/36.6 M	13.6	4.15
AT 180 FEET/54.9 M	7.0	2.13
VOLUME IGNORING BURNS	35,017 cubic feet	991 cubic meters

Wendell Flint at the Methuselah.

Methuselah Tree (#5 MH)

Mr. Hoskins probably named this and other trees such as the Adam around 1884. It is near the Bear Creek entrance to Mountain Home State Forest. After entering the forest from Springville, go past the side road to the left that goes to the forest headquarters. Turn right at the next turnoff, which quickly ends in an open space. There is a gate at the southeast corner of the open space. Follow the road through the gate and walk a few yards to the sign for the Methuselah Tree. When I first saw the tree around 1950 a new leader had grown out of a broken top to reach a height of 225 feet, but now the tree is again stubbed back. It lost its new leader by wind or lightning and is growing yet another leader.

Although not the largest tree in this forest, it is one of the most impressive. It has the largest base. At one time local enthusiasts thought this was the world's largest tree. The tree still has a respectable volume even though it was broken off at about 173 feet.

Mike and I measured this tree in 1989. I had made some measurements a few years earlier, but I did not get a good second transit line. N. E. Beckwith, who was on the Jourdan Team, may have also measured it around 1950. I know he mapped the base from a document that is stored at Sequoia National Park headquarters.

COMMENTARY BY MIKE LAW

When Wendell and I measured this tree, we calculated a height of 207.8 feet, ground perimeter of 95.8 feet, and breast height diameter of 24 feet. In June of 2002, Robert Van Pelt and I used a laser to take measurements from an angle that Wendell and I could not obtain with a transit. We were able to work through a clump of dogwood much closer to the tree. From this side the tree is much larger, 17 feet through at one hundred feet off the ground. The Methuselah is the remains of what was once a much larger tree, probably in the mid-forty thousand cubic foot range. The measurements Wendell and I took in 1989 provided a volume of 32,897 cubic feet. The new measurements indicate a volume of 34,000 to 37,000 cubic feet.

Allen Russell Tree (#6 MH)

This tree was dedicated by Tulare County in 1990 to Allen Russell, a Balch Park ranger, for his untiring efforts to make Balch Park a nice place to visit. Earlier, Russell had asked Mike and me to measure this tree. It looked big to him. Mike and I measured it in 1985. The tree has about one-half of its base burned away on the uphill side. It does not taper much. The tree is on the north side of the Balch Park Campground.

Allen Russell Tree dimensions:		
	ENGLISH	METRIC
HEIGHT	253.9 feet	77.38 meters
GROUND PERIMETER	79.7	24.29
DIAMETER: AT BREAST HIGH	21.7	6.61
AT 60 FEET/18.3 M	13.9	4.24
AT 120 FEET/36.6 M	13.2	4.02
AT 180 FEET/54.9 M	10.1	3.08
VOLUME IGNORING BURNS	31,606 cubic feet	895 cubic meters

Unnamed Tree (Three Fingered Jack) (#7 MH)

Mike and I were driving down the Mountain Home Road towards Balch Park when Mike saw something to the west. What we found was a very unusual tree. Its bark was smooth and pink on one side, but red and fluted on the other (see the Harlequin trees below). It was too small for our purposes. Down the old logging road to the south was another tree that did not look too promising, so we ignored it. Later we had a second look at it and saw that it was a fair sized tree after all. We decided to measure it. I refer to this tree as Three Fingered Jack because its dead top looks like a great, somewhat mutilated hand.

The tree is just outside the northern boundary of Balch Park. If you leave Balch Park going north, look for an old road running southward on the west side of the Mountain Home Road just after leaving the park. This old logging road will lead to the Harlequin trees. Beyond that, at a sharp bend in the road, is Three Fingered Jack. The base of the tree has been reduced in half by fire. There is a short tunnel through the tree on its south side. It has some large limbs and leans a bit. Mike and I measured the tree in 1992.

Three Fingered Jack dimensions:		
	ENGLISH	METRIC
HEIGHT	239.9 feet	73.12 meters
GROUND PERIMETER	82.5	25.14
DIAMETER:AT BREAST HIGH	18.6	5.67
AT 60 FEET/18.3 M	13.9	4.24
AT 120 FEET/36.6 M	13.3	4.05
AT 180 FEET/54.9 M	11.4	3.47
VOLUME IGNORING BURNS	30,118 cubic feet	853 cubic meters

Other Large Sequoia Sights in the Mountain Home Grove

Five Sisters (#8 MH)

A magnificent cluster of five sequoias at the end of the road that runs just to the south of the Adam Tree.

Harlequin Trees (# 9 MH)

Found on the way to Three Fingered Jack as described above. These trees have very unusual bark. One side is smooth and pink, the other is fluted and red.

The Hercules Tree.

Hercules Tree (#10 MH)

Jesse Hoskings cut a 12 by 12 by 12-foot room out of this tree for a shelter. It leaked. He made it into a trinket shop for sequoia wood curios. The tree has suffered some recent indignities. The door to the room was swiped. Someone threw a live cigarette butt on the ground near the tree and heavily damaged the tree. Then some fool lit a fire in the room itself, and further harm was done.[2]

Great Bonsai Tree (#11 MH)

This is one of the great sequoia sights to be seen anywhere. Follow the Dogwood Meadow Road to the point where it turns sharply south to the Genesis Tree. Then walk the heavily obstacle-strewn road (to prevent people from trying to drive it) to the top of the ridge. Then proceed north along the ridge for about 300 yards. On a pile of rocks is a monstrous sequoia with many huge limbs almost extending to the ground. Although not one of the very large trees, this short sequoia has no equal in visual impact. There is reason to think this is an old, old tree.

Lady Alice Tree (#12 MH)

You'll find her in Balch Park, just south of the Hollow Log. This is a fine specimen.

Old Jobe (#13 MH)

Old Jobe is the remains of a very large fire-reduced tree. At one time it might have been the largest tree in the grove.

Oliver Twist (#14MH)

On the north side of the Summit Road and just south of Balch Park, this tree has a spiral bark pattern.

Old Jobe.

Wishbone Tree (#15 MH)

The Wishbone is found on a self-guided nature trail leaving the Bear Hill Road just south of the turnoff to Dogwood Meadow. In about 1886, John J. Doyle built a road to this tree at Summer Home, now Balch Park. Traces of the old road are still visible near the tree.[2]

There are several fine groups of smaller sequoias. One is on a trail west of Shake Camp. The other can be reached by taking the trail across from the Frazier Campground northward for about three-quarters of a mile (#16 MH & #19 MH).

Centennial Stump (#17 MH)

Located just west of the Enterprise Mill site on the north side of the road, this was said to be the biggest tree in the world before it was cut down for exhibition purposes. It was claimed to be 300 feet tall and 111 feet around on the ground. An 1886 map of Tulare County said the tree had a diameter of 46 feet. My measurements seem to indicate that this is an exaggeration. The maximum diameter on top of the present stump is 24 feet and it is 86.9 feet around on the ground. A ring count showed the tree was 3,000 years old. I doubt it. However, a nearby stump has a ring count of over 3,000 years according to dendrologists from Arizona State University.[3]

Eve Tree (#18 MH)

Look for Eve just north of the Adam on the same trail. It was killed when its bark was stripped for display at some fair. The project was never finished. The intruders also tried to cut the tree down. They failed in this as well. This naked Eve is not such a hot item now, but you may want to see it out of curiosity.

Hollow Log (#20 MH)

Clinton T. Brown noted this naturally fallen tree in 1870.[4] It is just past the entrance to Balch Park.

Nero Tree (#21 MH)

John Mckiearnan cut this tree down in 1903 for exhibition purposes - from its hollow inside! The tree fell into a pile of useless rubble.[5] What is left of it is found in the Frazier Campground.

Sawed Tree (#22 MH)

This tree is found east of the Russell Tree in Balch Park on a road looping the campgrounds. Paul Sheppa bought the tree for twenty dollars in 1881. It was nearly sawed through and wedged to make it fall. It didn't. This apparently made Paul nervous, so he went away.

Alder Creek Grove

This fine medium sized grove is across the Middle Fork of the Tule River to the southeast of the Mountain Home Grove. It is reached by a good road called Redwood Drive, which leaves Highway 190 from a point east of Camp Nelson. It is about 6.5 miles from Highway 190. There are many old logging roads in the grove, making it easy to see. The heart of the grove is

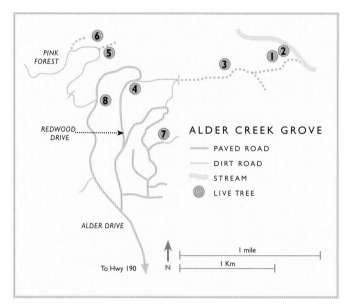

1. Amos Alonzo Stagg 2. Big base tree 3. Large tree 4. Window tree
5. Large tree 6. Large pink tree 7. Large snag 8. Large backyard tree

in private hands. The Sequoia National Forest owns perhaps 238 acres on the west side of the grove. The total grove area may be as much as 733 acres.

Amos Alonzo Stagg (#1 AC)

L. Day noticed this tree in 1931. Day, N. E. Beckwith (of the Jourdan Team) and one other person (whose name I do not know) measured it in 1932. However, they left three sets of measurements that do not agree very well. The story goes that Beckwith fell ill on this trip and left the final measurements to the other two. Some of their measurements seem to match those of another tree, rather than the Stagg. This is the only really large giant sequoia still in private hands.

To find the tree, take Redwood Drive north through the Sequoia Crest area to its northernmost point where the road turns west and then south. From this point, take the dirt road heading east. Soon you will find a locked gate with a sign granting revocable permission to enter private land. It is OK, as of this writing, to proceed to an old cabin site. To the east of a cabin, the old road will continue to a fork in the road. Take the left trail a few hundred yards to a sign pointing out the trail to the Stagg, which will be to the left downhill. A short walk on this trail will take you to the base of the tree.

Stagg Tree dimensions:		
	ENGLISH	METRIC
HEIGHT	243.0 feet	74.06 meters
GROUND PERIMETER	109.0	33.22
DIAMETER: AT BREAST HIGH	22.8	6.95
AT 60 FEET/18.3 M	18.2	5.55
AT 120 FEET/36.6 M	15.0	4.57
AT 180 FEET/54.9 M	12.5	3.81
VOLUME IGNORING BURNS	42,557 cubic feet	1,205 cubic meters

The Amos Alonzo Stagg.

The tree was named around 1960 for Amos Alonzo Stagg when Sequoia Crest was developed for cabin sites. Stagg was a famous football coach at the University of Chicago, and then at the University of the Pacific in Stockton, California. He was also noted as a great humanitarian by the students who knew him.

The lower trunk is magnificent, very heavy, and with a rich red-brown color. The top has a sizable room burned out of it, complete with an entry, a window, and a flue. The room was discovered in the autumn of 1993 when a group of tree climbers from Georgia went to the top in a snowstorm. There is a large burn at the base on the uphill side and there is a short tunnel forming a flying buttress.

Mike and I have measured this tree several times, most recently in 1977. I rate it as the sixth largest tree.

Other Interesting Trees in the Alder Creek Grove

There is an unnamed tree a few hundred yards north of the Stagg, on the south edge of the South Fork of Alder Creek (#2 AC). This tree has a truly immense base due to a very large basal buttress that extends to the steep bank of the creek. It is almost a vertical drop from this buttress to the creek below. In 1977, I was able to put a tape around the tree at ground level, and to get two base diameters. By the way, do NOT try to walk around this tree. 'Tain't safe. Some hiking friends of mine, Bob and Paula Graham, both with a weakness for climbing things, did it a few years ago. It took them a half hour! There is no trail to the tree. It can be reached by clambering through the brush starting at the Stagg Tree, being careful not to get into the watershed to the west.

When I first saw the tree there was a shingle nailed high on the trunk with a name on it, but I couldn't read it. Maybe it was the original Day Tree (see the Stagg Tree). The tree sits on steep ground, has a dead snag for a top, and does not look too imposing from the uphill side. But from the downhill side – wow! It is an amazing 155 feet around on the ground, about 20 feet in diameter at breast high (a guess), which is perhaps at the 20 foot level above the down-hill side. It is 57 feet across the buttresses on the level and it is 43.6 feet measuring up the slope, which is steep. We have considered measuring it since there is an outside chance it has a trunk volume around 30,000 cubic feet.

There is another large unnamed tree to be found west of the cabin site mentioned above (#3 AC). Its top can be seen from this area. An old trail leads downhill to it. It is 106.8 feet around on the ground, but only 65.4 feet around on the level at the highest point of the ground. The tree has a broken, many-limbed top, is not very tall, and is too small at 60 feet to be a really large tree. A shadow measurement gave a diameter of 12.1 feet for this level.

There are other interesting trees in this grove. One is the only living example of a weeping sequoia living in the forest. Other weeping sequoias are cultivated in nurseries. The branches of this tree fall directly downward, so that the tree is a skinny column. It is a juvenile tree, and since it is so rare and so easily harmed, I'm not saying where it is.

There is a window tree near the bend in the road at the north end of Redwood Drive (#4 AC). There are several trees with plaques at their base commemorating them to various people. There is a great ruin of a tree just east of the cabins (#7 AC).

A dirt road leads from Alder Drive into the Forest Service part of the grove. The road is dirt and steep – it is best to walk it. There is a huge tree (but not quite big enough to measure) just behind the area where some old remnants of machinery are found (#5 AC). Also seen here are several harlequin trees – half red fluted bark and half smooth pink bark. After this, the road makes a sharp bend westward, then southward. Below this point are the remains of a parallel logging road. Along this road is a forest of silvery pink barked sequoias, up to forty of them. I call this area the "Pink Forest." There are a couple of large ones at the east end of this area (#6 AC). The other pink trees are relatively small. There is a huge tree in someone's backyard. It has a diameter of 20 feet breast high. Don't encroach – this is a private home. Gawk at it from the road. It may be the largest backyard tree in the world (#8 AC).

Belknap Complex of Groves (McIntyre Grove)

Most groves are pretty well defined. This one is not. It has four almost disconnected lobes, and a separate unit in the canyon to the south. There are also isolated groups of trees separate from the main population. Four of the large areas have been named as groves. The Belknap Grove lies on the northwest slope of a ridge, south of the south fork of the middle fork of the Tule River. The eastern part of the grove is known as the Wheel Meadow Grove. From a point below the

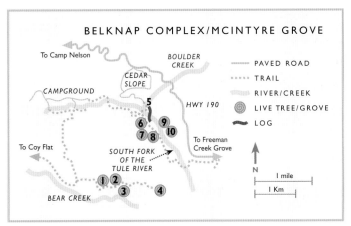

1. Patriarch 2. Broken tree 3. Fire-reduced tree 4. Pink trees
5. Teeter-totter log 6. Tunneled tree 7. Old Knot Head 8. Bent Tree
9. Gutless Goliath 10. Near Gutless Giant

cabins at Cedar Slope, the trees are confined to a narrow band down the river. This has been called the McIntyre Grove. Higher on the hill to the south is an unnamed lobe of the grove. Isthmuses of trees connect all these lobes. The canyon to the south is fairly well separated from the rest of the complex and consists of several groups of trees along Bear Creek. This is the Carr Wilson Grove. This whole complex, excluding the Carr Wilson, has also been called the McIntyre Grove. The main complex can be reached by Highway 190. One way is to turn off to Camp Nelson, then take the road to the Belknap Campground and go to its end. A good trail then runs along the river, eventually exiting at Quaking Aspen Meadow, from where it is also possible to enter the grove. The grove can also be reached by a dirt road through Cedar Slope. This is a large area of giant sequoias covering about 1,500 acres. There are several areas within the grove that contain no sequoias. Most of this grove is within the Giant Sequoia National Monument. There are several interesting sequoias in this complex, one of which is of imposing size.

Patriarch (#1 BC-M)

A friend of a cabin owner in Camp Nelson named this tree about 1980. The tree is at the top edge of the grove. It can be reached by taking the Bear Creek Trail, whose trailhead is just south of the cabins in Coy Flat. It is about a four-mile hike to the tree. There is no mistaking it – it is clearly more massive than any other sequoia near it. There is a shorter but steeper trail to the tree just east of the Belknap Campground, not far from a bridge over the river formed by a fallen sequoia. This trail may be hard to follow. It is marked with beer can tops nailed to trees. The trail eventually intersects the Bear Creek Trail. The Patriarch is to the left about .25 miles.

Wendell Flint with large limb from Patriarch Tree.

It is a very short tree with many huge limbs. A few years ago, a really big limb broke off and knocked off two smaller limbs as well. These limbs lie south of the tree. You should take a good look at them. Before the limbs broke off, the tree had a crown spread of over 100 feet. The base is relatively small, but the trunk is very thick higher up.

Mike Law, Dennis Coggins, Robert Bergen, and I measured this tree in 1984. Our first effort was not too enjoyable. It was hot, and we hiked the Bear Creek Trail, which is uphill all the way. We got the transit located, then it started to rain, then hail, then there were nasty lightning strikes, some so close that the thunder seemed to come before the bolt! Dennis yelled,

The Patriarch Tree before losing large limb.

"Don't get out in the open – you'll be a target!" Mike said that being under a tree was a bad idea. Then it became a bad idea to not do anything because the hailstones became too big. What we did was certainly wrong, but it worked. I'm not saying what we did because it would be bad advice. Mike and I returned to the tree several weeks later to finish measuring.

Patriarch dimensions:		
	ENGLISH	METRIC
HEIGHT	176.4 feet	53.76 meters
GROUND PERIMETER	72.6	22.13
DIAMETER:AT BREAST HIGH	19.3	5.88
AT 60 FEET/18.3 M	16.6	5.06
AT 120 FEET/36.6 M	13.4	4.08
AT 180 FEET/54.9 M	--	
VOLUME IGNORING BURNS	30,020 cubic feet	850 cubic meters

Other Interesting Trees in the Complex

If you continue on the Bear Creek Trail eastward from the Patriarch, you will pass a large broken tree on the left, then just over the ridge, a fire reduced monster on the right. The trail goes through beautiful sequoias to a meadow surrounded by trees of the pink barked variety (#2, #3, #4 BC-M).

On the Nelson Trail going eastward from the Cedar Slope area, there are several sights to see. After passing through a fine group of trees, one can see a most unusual log (#5 BC-M). Here is a mature sequoia log that can actually be lifted! It is balanced so that if it is pushed rhythmically at its upper end it will move. I have made a fortune, uncollected of course, by betting I could lift the log. My cousin Robert has dubbed it the Teeter-totter Tree. Continuing on upstream, the trail goes through a drive-through tree (#6 BC-M). Apparently a logging road was cut years ago, and then the tunnel was widened later. After crossing a spring, and staggering a bit uphill, there is a little meadow. Beyond and to the south is a tree with a great knot growing out of the top with stunted foliage. We call it Old Knot Head (#7 BC-M). Nearby are three fallen trees, all knocked over by a single falling tree. We call these the Domino Trees. Farther east and just south of the trail is the most unusual Bent Tree (#8 BC-M). Sometime in the past, a lightning strike started a fire about halfway up the trunk, nearly burning it through. The top leaned but did not break. Apparently, healing has stabilized the tree. The cavity below the bend is still very evident.

Across the river to the north are two large sequoias that are not quite big enough to meet my standards (#9, #10 BC-M). The first one, which I call the Near Gutless Giant, is not far from the river. To the east, within eyeballing distance and uphill is the Gutless Goliath, a tree that lost its lower parts to fire. It is quite heavy midtrunk and sports a tall dead spire for a top. It is well worth seeing if you don't mind fording the river and clambering up a steep bank.

Robert Bergen and I checked out a rumor that there was a really big one in the Carr Wilson unit. We found it – it just wasn't big. There are some odd looking sequoias in this unit with pale bark and lighter than usual foliage.

Black Mountain Grove

This very large grove is misnamed. It is not on Black Mountain, which is to the west. It lies near Solo Peak. The grove can be reached by driving on a partly hard-topped, partly dirt road. From Highway 190, at the first Camp Nelson turnoff, take the road that goes through Coy Flat. After four miles, there are some cabins in a logged area. Beyond that the road branches – the road on the left goes into the Tule Indian Reservation. Take Forest Service Road 21S12 to the right. The section of grove to the north of Solo Peak is mostly in Giant Sequoia National Monument. There are some private areas that were logged of sequoias about 100 years ago.

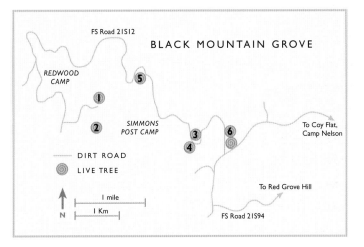

1. Black Mountain Beauty 2. Blasted Mammoth 3. Harlequin Tree
4. Large tree 5. Large tree with small base 6. Large tree

To the south of Solo Peak, the grove is on Indian land and some privately owned in-holdings. The whole grove may cover as much as 2,500 acres. There is at least one tree that exceeds 30,000 cubic feet, plus a number of interesting trees. There are no formal trails, but there are a number of old logging roads that can be easily walked.

Black Mountain Beauty (#1 BM)

Mike brought this tree to my attention around 1983. It is a gorgeous specimen with a relatively small base, but tapers little from bottom to top. It has abundant foliage, and since the non-sequoia trees have been logged around it, one can see the whole tree. It can be reached from Forest Service Road 21S12 by keeping right on the road (ignoring a short spur that goes to a trailhead) to the edge of the cut over area. The road is dirt and can be rough. Walking north-ward down a partially overgrown logging road and over a hump or so, the tree comes into view. The name is unofficial, but Mike and I like it (#1 BM). Mike and I measured it in 1986.

Black Mountain Beauty dimensions:		
	ENGLISH	METRIC
HEIGHT	262.7 feet	80.07 meters
GROUND PERIMETER	75.8	23.10
DIAMETER: AT BREAST HIGH	19.1	5.82
AT 60 FEET/18.3 M	15.1	4.60
AT 120 FEET/36.6 M	11.7	3.57
AT 180 FEET/54.9 M	10.3	3.14
VOLUME IGNORING BURNS	32,224 cubic feet	912 cubic meters

Other Notable Trees in the Black Mountain Grove

The remains of what may have been the largest tree in this grove are found on top of a hill. The road to the Black Mountain Beauty area makes a sharp turn to the north. Hiking from the bend it is cross-country to the top of the hill (#2 BM). Although this tree is alive, it is broken off about 90 feet up. It has a ground perimeter of 96.9 feet and has a breast height diameter of 22 feet. Its unofficial name is the Blasted Mammoth.

A large unnamed tree, with smooth pink bark on one side and red fluted bark on the other, is near a sharp turn in the road about a mile from the first snow gate (#3 BM). I call it the Harlequin Tree. It is one of the larger ones of this kind. On the other side of the road just up the hill is a large imposing tree (#4 BM).

The forest service road passes by a high dirt bluff. Park here and walk northward to a large sequoia on the right. Then climb the road cut to the right past this tree, and proceed about 100 yards to a well hidden, imposing tree. It has a very small base for such a big tree. Its midtrunk is heavy (#5 BM).

There are other trees in this grove that approach being big ones, but all taper too much. One such tree is a handsome specimen visible from Forest Service Road 21S12 not far from where this road branches to the north on the east side of the road (#6 BM). There are at least two large sequoias on the Tule Indian Reservation. Permission must be granted from the reservation to enter this area.

Mike and the Snake

We spotted two large trees on top of the ridge above Simmons Post Pile (See BM map). Mike decided to look at them. I took one look at the long, brushy terrain he planned to go through, and I decided to snooze in the car and await his return. Mike plunged into the brush with a lot of verve. About fifteen minutes later, I heard a great crashing sound up the hill. This noise continued until a pooped out Mike struggled down to the road. It seems that he was stepping over a log when he spied a huge rattlesnake glaring at him from the point where his foot was about to land. I think he levitated, then turned tail and fled down the mountain. This was a very unusual snake because Mike has told this story a number of times over the years, and the snake has grown to a most imposing size.

Tule River Watershed

Is there a Champion in the Tule River Watershed? There are a number of groves in this area that are not discussed above. Perhaps something may turn up in one of them. Dwight Willard and Bob Rogers visited the Maggie Mountain Grove and found no big ones. Dr. and Mrs. Graham and Bob Rogers visited the out-of-the-way Burro Creek Grove. They found some imposing specimens, but no super giant. I have seen no oversized trees in the Red Hill or Peyrone Groves. There are parts of the three large groves mentioned above that I have yet to see. Offhand, I think the Tule River Watershed is the best place to track down a new champion – if one exists.

Freeman Creek Grove. Photograph by Dick Burns

Chapter 6:
THE KERN AND OTHER SOUTHERN WATERSHEDS

With the exception of the Freeman Creek Grove, these groves are small to medium sized. There are some very large trees in these groves, but there are no real challengers for the championship.

Freeman Creek Grove

There are two main accesses to this fabulous grove. From the west, take the first surfaced road east from the north end of the Quaking Aspen area from Highway 190. About one-third of a mile to the east is a dirt road. This road immediately forks. Take the left fork to a parking space for the trail to the Freeman Creek Grove. There is a trailhead sign for trail 33E20 that goes to Lloyd Meadow. Keep right on the trail. From the east, the grove can be reached by paved Road 22S82 from Johnsondale. There is a wide place to park by a pair of sequoia logs on the west side of the road after passing Pyle's Boys Camp. Informal trails lead to the grove from there.

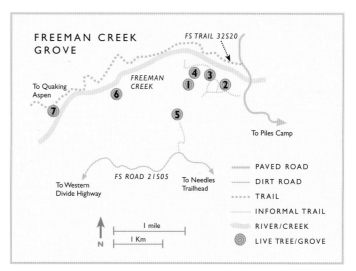

1. Great Goshawk 2. Large tree 3. Ride Through Tree 4. Telescope Tree 5. Loren's Tree 6. Unnamed 7. Bannister's Tree

This large grove covers about 1,800 acres in the Freeman Creek watershed. This area is a botanical reserve under the Sequoia National Forest administration except for one small private plot. It contains at least one tree whose trunk volume is greater than 30,000 cubic feet. This is one of the least disturbed groves outside of the national parks.

Great Goshawk Tree (#1 FC)

Bill and Carol Croft led me to the Great Goshawk Tree in 1990. It was so-called by Bill, because when he ran across the tree in 1988, an angry goshawk that had a nest in the top of a dead snag sequoia, swooped down upon him.

This tree was inventoried by the Evans Dwyer-Rucker survey in 1935/1936.[1] According to the forester of Sequoia National Forest, Douglas Leisz, this tree was the largest in the survey at the time the lower part of the grove was added to the national forest.[2]

There is no maintained trail to the tree. Behind the fallen logs by the road mentioned above, there is an informal trail to the west. The first tree of note is a large specimen with a peculiar top (#2 FC). Here the trail branches – both go to the tree. On the south branch of the trail, there is a pair of trees very close together. The north tree is dead. The trail crosses boggy ground and eventually goes through the Ride Through Tree (#3 FC), a tree with a massive base. After that, the trail crosses a rocky area and continues to a meadow-like area. Leave the trail and follow the watershed southward to the left. Continue to a sequoia log laying across the drainage, cross the drainage on your right, then go on to three or four old dead sequoia snags on the west side of the drainage. The Great Goshawk is to the east just on the other side of the drainage. The forest is dense here, so the tree is easy to miss.

This is probably the largest tree in this grove. The lower trunk is very impressive. There is an extensive deep burn on the uphill side. When I first saw this tree, I noted that there was mud caked inside the burn to a height of at least 30 feet. This was a great puzzle. I also noted that several of the surrounding sequoias were also mud spattered. Forest Clingan of Dunlap near Grant Grove, a long time giant sequoia fan, supplied me with the solution to this mystery. He said that occasionally a huge downdraft of wind will hit the earth with great force, in this case stripping the soil of its cover and splattering the underlying mud all about.[3] I was a bit skeptical until I read an account of several abodes near Biola, a San Joaquin Valley hamlet, being destroyed in this manner. The phenomenon is real.

Great Goshawk dimensions:		
	ENGLISH	METRIC
HEIGHT	255.2 feet	77.78 meters
GROUND PERIMETER	90.2	27.49
DIAMETER: AT BREAST HIGH	23.1	7.04
AT 60 FEET/18.3 M	14.6	4.45
AT 120 FEET/36.6 M	13.7	4.18
AT 180 FEET/54.9 M	9.3	2.83
VOLUME IGNORING BURNS	32,783 cubic feet	928 cubic meters

Just to the north of the Goshawk is a great Telescope Tree, the most impressive tree of its kind I have seen (#4 FC). It would be in sight of the Goshawk if it weren't for the thick forest. It is so huge that the last time I looked at it, there was a juvenile sequoia growing inside of it! Crawl inside this tree and gawk at the sky above. This tree is known as the Castro Tree to "honor" some graffiti carver. My cousin Robert Bergen, Mike Law, Jerry Latham, and I measured the Goshawk in 1990.

Other Possible Big Ones

Loren's Tree (#5 FC)

There is a large tree in the same watershed as the Great Goshawk, but high up in the grove to the south. No measurements have been taken except for a few shadow measurements and a perimeter. It is called Loren's Tree after Loren Ross, an independent sequoia searcher who identified it as "large." In 1991, Loren Ross, Bill Croft, his wife Carol, and I paid this tree a visit. I pooped out and had to spend some time sitting on a rock, where I sulked a bit because my old legs refused to work properly. However, the others obtained tape and shadow measurements. The ground perimeter was 73.3 feet and the breast high diameter was 19.4 feet. The main stem of the tree seemed to be heavy and the height was average. It could possibly contain 30,000 cubic feet of trunk volume.

Unnamed (#6 FC)

Another tree of similar size is found just across Freeman Creek to the south if one uses the west entry into the grove. The trail makes a few switchbacks as it descends into a major part of the grove about a mile from the grove's entry. This unnamed tree is 62.4 feet around on the ground and has a breast high diameter of only 17.8 feet; but like Loren's Tree, the trunk is a cylinder. It is barely possible that its trunk could contain as much as 30,000 cubic feet.

Bannister's Tree (#7 FC)

From the trailhead of 33S20, walk downstream for about .8 miles to the first sequoias. If you are not paying attention, you will miss a remarkable group of very large trees. The trail crosses a little watershed that drains into Freeman Creek. Hop across it, continue on the trail for maybe 50 yards more, and then go downhill. Just north of the Freeman Creek, you will find the remains of a huge sequoia, known as the Freeman Snag, Bannister's Tree, or Sequoia Yah.

In 1926, A. W. Bannister of Bakersfield reported that he had found a tree that was 300 feet tall. He said it was 119 feet around and that it was 40 feet across. The tree was about 11 miles east of Camp Nelson. He called it the Sequoia Yah. Weldon Heald of the Sierra Club checked out a tree that he thought was the largest in the area, but he found it was only 69.6 feet around at a point a little lower than breast high. I found it to be 67.5 feet around at breast height. This figure agrees well with Heald's. When I first saw the tree, there was a large AB carved in soft bark. These initials are almost impossible to see now because the bark has sloughed off. A few years after Bannister's discovery, there was (I think) a forest fire that burned the top out of this tree. It is still 26,100 cubic feet of trunk volume. Within a short distance from the Bannister are several large and handsome trees, some leaners that seem about to fall, a telescope tree from which the sky can be seen from the inside, and a tree with spectacular limbs.

Long Meadow Grove

Although this grove has no super giants, there are a number of impressive trees that are very easy to see. There is a self-guided trail that takes you past the important trees in the lower part of the grove. This trail has a hard surface, is fairly level and is wheelchair accessible. This is a medium sized grove covering about 290 acres within the Giant Sequoia National Monument. A parking space is provided for a fee.

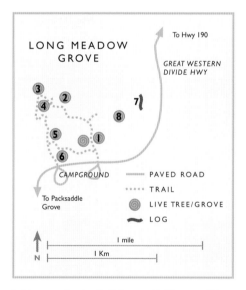

1. Unnamed pair 2. Tall tree 3. Group of five
4. Hungry sequoia 5. Spike 6. Large tree
7. Remains 8. Red Chief

Unnamed Pair (#1 LM)

If one takes the loop trail counterclockwise, the trail will go between two imposing trees. One has a very peculiar bent top – the higher up, the more it bends.

Tall Tree (#2 LM)

This large tree to the right of the trail has an interesting branch that hangs almost straight down.

Group of Five (#3 LM)

This is a close group of five trees, three of which are growing together.

Hungry Sequoia (#4 LM)

After crossing the stream, you will find a hungry sequoia "devouring" an incense cedar.

Large Tree (#5 LM)

A little farther on and across a small meadow to the left is the largest tree in this area. I call it Spike.

Another Big One (#6 LM)

Another large tree located near the main road, is on the branch of the trail that leads to the south unit of the campground.

Remains (#7 LM)

A second branch of the trail (incomplete as of 1998) looping to the right and back has the remains of what may have been the grove's largest tree. There is a large fallen sequoia to inspect.

Red Chief (#8 LM)

The largest tree in the grove does not have a trail to it. It is in the southwest corner of the grove. It is distinguished by a large knot on one side. It is in an area that has been logged of nearly all non-sequoia trees. When Mike and I went to measure it, deer flies made us miserable, so we called it the Deer Fly Tree. When it looked as if it had a volume of over 30,000 cubic feet, Mike renamed it Red Chief. After it proved to be smaller than 30,000 cubic feet, Mike no longer cared what it was called.

Packsaddle Grove

This is a very nice medium sized grove covering about 325 acres in the Giant Sequoia National Monument. It can be reached by taking the Western Divide Highway, then turning east on Road SM50 (also reached via Johnsondale). Then turn on the mostly dirt Road 23S16. This will take you to the west side of the grove. Most of the grove lies on the east side of the road. There are two good entry points. One is at the north end of the grove where the first sequoias are seen. The northern part of the grove is to the east. At the south end of Packsaddle Meadow is a gated road to the east. One can park near the gate, walk the road for perhaps .3 miles and then drop over the ridge top into drainages that contain the giants.

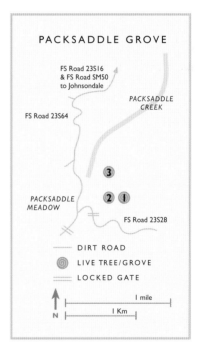

1. Ghost 2. Packsaddle Giant
3. Candelabra

The Ghost Tree Rumors Solved

If you don't mind, I'll digress a bit. This is how my quest to find the biggest tree really began. My uncle, John Bergen, gave me his December 1935 issue of *Field and Stream* with an article by Joe Mears about a fishing trip in this part of the woods.[4] He recounted the tale of the "Ghost Tree" (#1 PS). He said that Charley Tebbetts, a hunter, probably found the tree around 1885. Guy Hughs, in an article in the *Bakersfield Californian* in 1961, said that Jim Pasco, Jim Dunlap, and Tom Baker had found the tree in 1885. This broken tree measured, according to them, 120 feet around.[5] Hughs also said he located it sometime between 1912 and 1916. He also said it was 120 feet around. Bill Calkins, a fisherman, claimed that he had rediscovered the tree in 1931. However, John Guthrie, a local cattleman, was involved in the Hughs' discovery and in Calkins' finding of the tree. Guthrie didn't seem to recall that Hughs found the tree to be 120 feet around.[6] Calkins denied that the tree had ever been "lost." The June 1961 issue of the *Los Angeles Times* carried an article about this tree called "Foresters Out on a Limb: Is There a Ghost Tree?" In it was listed possible finders including the ones mentioned above. It also said people coming from French Joe to the Packsaddle area had encountered the tree from time to time. However, the private owners of this area at that time had inventoried the sequoias and found no such tree.

Another rumor possibly involving the Ghost Tree was published in the *Daily Alta Californian* in 1879. It seems that Mark Kern had found a tree 15 miles from Kernville. He said he measured this tree with a rope and found it to be 135 feet around at 5 feet above ground level.[7]

When I first reported my measurements of the Packsaddle Giant to the Forest Service in 1950, I received a reply asking whether I had seen a tree that was supposed to be 124.5 feet around the trunk. It was assumed to be in a grove east of the Packsaddle Grove. I have looked for it several times, and all I have found was a rather widely spaced double tree. Cunningham, who was forest superintendent at the time it was supposed to have been found, declared that it was a double tree and that he was a bit annoyed. It also turned out that this eastern grove was really continuous with the Packsaddle and not a separate grove.

In 1950, I started at Double Bunk and followed the trail to Packsaddle Meadow. Mears said that a white cloth had been tied to a tree that indicated which drainage the tree was in. The rag was still there! In no time, I was looking at the Ghost. A picture in the Mears article made identification a certainty that this was their Ghost Tree, which they named the Robert E. Lee.

Still there was something very wrong. In his article, Mears said that he and Bill Calkins had measured the girth of the tree at a point as high as they could reach. The picture showed them using the tape while standing atop a horse. He said it was 108 feet around. My measurement at breast height was 63 feet. The discrepancy is easily accounted for. Both Joe Mears and Bill Calkins were fishermen. In fact, the Mears article, *Big Trees and Big Fish*, is largely about fish.

Later, Bob Walker, and I may have solved the 108-foot mystery. His measurement can be arrived at if a nearly buried surface root is included. After all, although the picture showed the tree being measured high off the ground, Mears did not say that 108 feet was that measurement. Fishermen can be tricky.

From 1977 to 1986, we finally got good measurements on this tree after several tries, with Mike Law and Bob Walker helping. The tree is 180.6 feet to the top of the foliage, but it has been broken off at about 144 feet. It is 94.9 feet around at ground level, 20.7 feet at breast height, and 14.8 feet through at 60 feet. Beckwith had measured the tree, probably around 1951, and found it to be larger than I had. Perhaps he took but one transit line from the wide side. One thing is clear – it would have been quite a tree if it were complete.

Packsaddle Giant

Mears said in his *Big Trees and Big Fish* story that there was another large tree near the Ghost, but that it was badly burned and so it was not as large as the Ghost. There is such a specimen nearby, but clearly not the Ghost Tree. Almost in sight of the Ghost, a little farther down the drainage is a tree with a monstrous base. Although it is deeply burned, it is larger than the Ghost. Although it is not a tall tree, it is a more nearly complete tree, growing a new leader from a lightning blasted top. Mike and I call this tree the Packsaddle Giant (#2 PS). On my trip to find the Ghost Tree in 1950, I took notice of this imposing tree and made measurements each time I saw it. The tree has a great spreading base about 38 feet across a huge

Packsaddle Giant dimensions:		
	ENGLISH	METRIC
HEIGHT	218.0 feet	66.44 meters
GROUND PERIMETER	106.3	32.40
DIAMETER: AT BREAST HIGH	24.3	7.41
AT 60 FEET/18.3 M	14.4	4.39
AT 120 FEET/36.6 M	13.3	4.05
AT 180 FEET/54.9 M	8.5	2.59
VOLUME IGNORING BURNS	32,156 cubic feet	910 cubic meters

burned area. There are extending roots, making it difficult to decide what is tree trunk and what is exposed roots. Another problem is that the main trunk has a more or less triangular cross section, making mean diameters more difficult to calculate. This tree could well be the source of some of the rumors in this area. It is my opinion that this is the tree Mark Kern found. Mike and I gathered data on this tree from 1977 to 1990.

Candelabra

Mike and I saw a remarkable tree not too far from the Packsaddle Giant as early as 1971. We called it the Turnip Tree because it somehow reminded me of a huge turnip. In 1978, Bill Croft saw it and dubbed it the Candelabra Tree, a more fitting name (#3 PS). It has many large branches that lead to a great crown of foliage.

The tree can be found by starting at the Packsaddle Giant then continuing down its drainage to a creek a few hundred yards away. Go downstream to a point where the next drainage goes into the creek . . . and there it is. Actually, it is just over the ridge from the Packsaddle Giant. This tree looks larger than it is, and is impressive from the downhill side. Mike and I measured this tree around 1980. The Candelabra is 205.5 feet high with 26,341 cubic feet of wood.

Other Rumors

There were supposed to be some very big ones in the Parker Peak Grove and in the North Cold Spring Grove. A resident of the Tule Indian Reservation guided Mike and me to these trees in 1990. These were large trees, but not super giants. I have not found any oversized trees in the Red Hill Grove. Forest Supervisor Cunningham said there was a fair sized tree in the Deer Mill Creek.[8] I found it. It wasn't big. I also found nothing oversized in the Peyrone Grove. The newly recognized South Peyrone Grove could be a place to look.

Wendell Flint and Dennis Coggins examine the Ghost Tree.

Mike Law and Wendell Flint have taken their love of sequoia to canvas, producing numerous paintings.
Big Tree Grove (top) by Wendell Flint. Giant Sequoia Meadow (bottom) by Mike Law.

Michael Taylor poses in front of the Del Norte Titan. Photograph by Ron Hildebrant.

Chapter 7:

COAST REDWOODS

What is the difference?

California has two species of trees that have specimens that exceed every other tree in the world in trunk volume. The giant sequoia, *Sequoiadendron giganteum*, is in the Sierra Nevada. Another name for the sequoia now going out of favor is the common name "sierra redwood." It has also been called "Big Tree" and "mammoth tree." The giant sequoia habitat extends from west of Lake Tahoe to southern Tulare County in more or less discrete groves. The coastal redwood, *Sequoia sempervirens*, occurs in the coastal ranges of California from San Luis Obispo County's northern line to the Oregon border and slightly beyond.

MAXIMUM HEIGHT
Giant sequoia — Up to 311 feet/94.8 meters.
Coastal redwood — Up to 370 feet/112.8 meters.

MAXIMUM DIAMETER
Giant sequoia — Up to 29 feet/8.8 meters.
Coastal redwood — Up to 25 feet/7.6 meters.

AGE
Giant sequoia — Up to approximately 3,200 years.
Coastal redwood — Up to approximately 2,200 years.

BARK
Giant sequoia — Brownish red, often deeply fluted.
Coastal redwood — Reddish chocolate brown, moderate fluting. May appear gray.

FOLIAGE
Giant sequoia — Awl shaped scale about 1/4 inch.
Coastal redwood — Short alternating needles about .6 inches long in 2 rows, some scale-like foliage.

ROOTS
Giant sequoia — Up to 6 feet deep. Usually up to 150 feet long.
Coastal redwood — Up to 4 feet deep. Usually up to 100 feet long.

CONE
Giant sequoia — 3 inches long.
Coastal redwood — Up to 1 inch long.

This book deals mainly with my search for the largest giant sequoias. I have done little looking for big coastal redwoods. The data I provide for the size of giant coastal redwoods depends on the measurements of others, and recently, with more modern instruments than I have used to measure the sequoias.[1]

Ron Hildebrant claims to have found redwoods as old as 4,000 years or more. He found an error in his methodology and at this time has declared the data on his "oldest" trees not valid. In 2001, Michael Taylor and Chris Atkins verified, by careful Impulse laser measurements, that one giant sequoia in the Redwood Mountain Grove is 311.4 feet tall.

Apparently, the search for the biggest of the coastal redwoods has been sporadic in the past and measurements taken have not been too reliable. There had been rumors of fallen trees such as the Big Tree of Maple Creek that was claimed to be larger than the General Sherman, and a tree near Arcata reputed to contain 90,000 cubic feet; but the largest known standing trees just don't compete with the largest giant sequoias. A number of people who were fond of redwoods, such as Dr. Robert Van Pelt, Michael Taylor, Steve Sillett, and Ron Hildebrant began to clearify our notion of what a really big redwood is like. I am grateful for the data they have supplied; this chapter would have been impossible without their help. I have done no more than stretch a tape around a few of them and take a shadow measurement or so.

Jedediah Smith Redwoods State Park

Del Norte Titan (Largest redwood)

This enormous redwood was found by Michael Taylor and Steve Sillett in July 1998. They call that day their "Day of Discovery" because they also discovered other giants not far away. They also named the tree. Perhaps others, including Frank Fox, recognized this tree to be of great size, but it was not measured.

Del Norte Titan dimensions:		
	ENGLISH	METRIC
HEIGHT	307 feet	93.57 meters
DIAMETER BREAST HEIGHT	23.7	7.22
VOLUME	36,893 cubic feet	1,045 cubic meters

Lost Monarch (Third largest redwood)

This most impressive tree was recognized and named by Michael Taylor and Steve Sillett on their Day of Discovery.

Lost Monarch dimensions:		
	ENGLISH	METRIC
HEIGHT	320 feet	97.53 meters
DIAMETER BREAST HEIGHT	26.0	7.92
VOLUME	34,914 cubic feet	989 cubic meters

Howland Hill Giant (Fourth largest redwood)

Dan Weyand, a ranger in Jedediah Smith Redwoods State Park, recognized this tree as being a big one in 1970. He called it the Weyand Tree. Others have called it the Howland Drive Tree and the Howland Hill Giant.

This tree is on the left side of Howland Drive going south in a bend of the road about .5 miles past the trailhead of the Boy Scout Tree. Although it lacks the huge base of the Titan or the Monarch, it still keeps its diameter well up toward the top – perhaps the most massive redwood of all above 180 feet. It has been measured by both Ron Hildebrant and Dr. Van Pelt. The two sets of figures do not conflict. I have seen the tree and put a tape around it at breast height. There is no conflict with the new measurements.

Looking up at the Howland Hill Giant. Photograph by Ron Hildebrant.

Howland Hill Giant dimensions:		
	ENGLISH	METRIC
HEIGHT	330 feet	100.58 meters
DIAMETER BREAST HEIGHT	19.1	5.82
VIB WITH ALL LEADERS	33,581 cubic feet	951 cubic meters

El Viejo Del Norte (Sixth largest redwood)

This is the third tree found by Taylor and Sillett on their Day of Discovery. I do not know the exact location of this tree other than the fact that it is somewhere near the Del Norte Titan and the Lost Monarch trees. The tree was named by the discoverers because of its gnarly appearance.

El Viejo Del Norte dimensions:		
	ENGLISH	METRIC
HEIGHT	330 feet	100.58 meters
DIAMETER BREAST HEIGHT	23.0	7.01
VOLUME	32,644 cubic feet	924 cubic meters

Prairie Creek Redwoods State Park

Prairie Creek Redwoods State Park has a number of very large redwoods.

Sir Isaac Newton (Fifth largest redwood)

Michael Taylor found, and Ron Hildebrant recognized, this tree in 1991. Based on Taylor and Hildebrant's recommendation, the American Forestry Association recognized it as the largest redwood. It soon had competition. I am fairly sure I have seen this tree, but if I did, I should have been more impressed. It is found along Prairie Creek.

Sir Isaac Newton dimensions:		
	ENGLISH	METRIC
HEIGHT	299 feet	91.13 meters
DIAMETER BREAST HEIGHT	22.5	6.86
VOLUME	33,192 cubic feet	940 cubic meters

Terex Titan (Seventh largest redwood)

Michael Taylor found the Terex Titan in 1991.

Terex Titan dimensions:		
	ENGLISH	METRIC
HEIGHT	270 feet	82.29 meters
DIAMETER BREAST HEIGHT	23.0	7.01
VOLUME	32,384 cubic feet	917 cubic meters

Adventure Tree (Eighth largest redwood)

Michael Taylor identified this tree in 1990.

Adventure Tree dimensions:		
	ENGLISH	METRIC
HEIGHT	341 feet	103.93 meters
DIAMETER BREAST HEIGHT	16.5	5.03
VOLUME	32,140 cubic feet	910 cubic meters

Iluvatar Tree (Second largest redwood)

One can find this tree a short distance to the right as one drives up the Iluvatar Road from near the main Prairie Creek headquarters and campground. It was identified and named by Michael Taylor in 1991.

Iluvatar Tree dimensions:		
	ENGLISH	METRIC
HEIGHT	300 feet	91.43 meters
DIAMETER BREAST HEIGHT	20.5	6.25
VOLUME	36,473 cubic feet	1,033 cubic meters

Newton B. Drury Tree (Eleventh largest redwood)

This tree is not far from the north end of Prairie Creek Redwoods. It is a short distance west of the main road through the park. Dr. Van Pelt and Michael Taylor, who identified and named this tree in 1990, have found it to have a trunk volume of 30,000 cubic feet. The Drury Tree has a lower trunk that lacks taper. It actually swells a bit as it goes up. Some calculations of volume place it slightly over 30,000 cubic feet. I doubt if any system of measurement can come closer than within +/- 500 cubic feet.

I'll also mention the Big Tree of Prairie Creek, a multiple-topped tree whose volume does not reach 30,000 cubic feet. This tree is a major sight in the park.

Humboldt Redwoods State Park and Redwood National Park

Bull Creek Giant (Ninth largest redwood)

This tree is about a mile downstream from the parking area at Bull Creek Flat. It was identified and named by Michael Taylor in 1992.

Bull Creek Giant dimensions:		
	ENGLISH	METRIC
HEIGHT	337 feet	102.71 meters
DIAMETER BREAST HEIGHT	21.0	6.40
VOLUME	31,144 cubic feet	882 cubic meters

The Stratosphere Giant, world's tallest tree. Photograph by Ron Hildebrant.

ARCO Giant (Tenth largest redwood)

This tree is found south of Prairie Creek Redwoods State Park headquarters and campground on Redwood National Park land. It is a very asymmetrical tree with huge limbs.

ARCO Giant dimensions:		
	ENGLISH	METRIC
HEIGHT	262 feet	79.85 meters
DIAMETER BREAST HEIGHT	22.5	6.86
VOLUME	30,699 cubic feet	869 cubic meters

How Tall are the Tallest Redwoods?

Below is a table of the tallest known trees. Note that there is little difference in their height. It has been my experience that height may be a figure that is less than accurate. The point where the axis of the tree meets the ground usually cannot be seen. Accumulation of forest litter around the base may pose a problem. For example, the giant sequoia Stagg, although its top is very dead, is at least a foot taller than it was twenty years ago. People walking around the tree have removed about a foot of forest duff.

Michael Taylor provided the numbers in the table of the ten tallest known trees given below from the data gathered by the *Tall Trees Club*, founded by Michael Taylor, Steve Sillett, Ron Hildebrant, and Dr. Robert Van Pelt.

TREE	LOCATION	HEIGHT	DIAMETER BREAST HEIGHT
Stratosphere Giant	HRSP	368.6 feet	17.0 feet
Mendocino Tree	MWSR	367.5	10.1
Paradox Tree	HRSP	367.1	12.8
National Geographic Tree	RNP	366.7	14.4
Federation Giant	HRSP	366.6	14.9
Harry Cole Tree	RNP	366.3	16.2
Pipe Dream Tree	HRSP	364.6	14.0
Millennium	HRSP	363.8	8.9
Lone Fern	HRSP	363.7	8.4
Swamp Tree	MSR	363.3	11.2

KEY TO LOCATIONS
MWSR Montgomery Woods State Reserve   RNP Redwood National Park
HRSP Humboldt Redwoods State Park

The Stratosphere Giant, world's tallest tree.
Photograph by Ron Hildebrant.

Are there Bigger Redwoods to be Found?

In all probability – yes. Although a very high percentage (about 96%) of the old growth redwood forest has been logged, there are many more old growth redwoods and a greater acreage of redwoods intact than for the sequoia. It is much easier to hide a monster redwood than a monster giant sequoia. The redwood forest is often a rainforest with dense masses of vegetation, as opposed to the giant sequoia groves, which are much more open. I was once bumbling around in a redwood forest and soon found that I had no idea where I was. It turned out I was within yards of my car! Rumors of big ones are not as common as with the giant sequoia. After a big redwood has been found, it is much harder to measure due to the density of the forest. Will someone find a redwood larger than the General Sherman? I doubt it.

Big tree hunter Wendell Flint (left) with Mike Law and Jerry Latham
start on a journey in search of another Big Tree.

The dense coast redwood forests may hold undiscovered
champion trees. Photograph by David Brothwell.

Appendix I: Measurement Terms

Diameters

Diameter is the length of a straight line through the center of an object. Several types of diameters are used for measuring big trees.

Mean Base Diameter

There are several methods of obtaining this figure, which is the mean diameter at the level of the mean base on the ground and projected on the level. The best way is to map the shape of the base and make calculations based on that. This method is seldom used. Another way is to find the geometric means of the long and short axes of the tree. I generally use a third method that gives good results. I use the geometric means of the ground perimeter and the perimeter at the high point of ground, and then divide the results by π (3.14159).

Maximum Base Diameter

This is the greatest diameter at the base of the tree. It should be taken on the level, but early tree measurers often took it on the slant. It is strictly a gee-whiz figure used mainly by old timers to boost the standing of their favorite candidate for the biggest tree in the world.

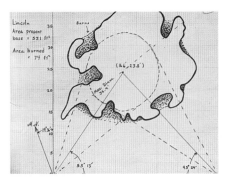

Mapping of the base of the Lincoln Tree.

Mean Diameter at High Point of Ground

Usually calculated by dividing the perimeter at the high point of ground by π.

Mean Diameter at Breast Height

Usually calculated by dividing the perimeter at breast height by π.

Mean Diameter at Other Levels

Strictly speaking, this is the geometric mean of at least two instrument measurements taken 90 degrees apart in direction and at the same height above the mean base. In practice this ideal is seldom reached. For the purpose of this book, I try to obtain as much significant data as I can from several lines, then interpolate (and occasionally extrapolate) the data so that means can be calculated for 30 feet, plus one at 16 feet. This has the advantage of making it easy to compare the size of one tree to another.

Height

Although height is the distance from the lowest to the highest point of an object, this measurement gets a bit more complicated when measuring trees. The ground is usually not level and the build-up of debris or wearing away of topsoil must be considered.

Tree height is the difference in elevation of the mean base level (the point where the axis of the main stem of the tree meets the ground) and the topmost point of the tree, be it foliage, a dead limb, or a live or dead main stem. Some trees are measured from the top of the foliage and the top of the stem for the purpose of volume calculation. Coastal redwoods are measured from a little different lower point, i. e. the point where the axis of the greatest ground diameter meets the axis of the least ground diameter. Usually this is of no great consequence since the point in question is usually unavailable for direct measurement. Interpret heights as accurate to within a foot to be safe.

Perimeters

Perimeter is a measurement of the outer boundary of an object. Several perimeter calculations are used for measuring trees.

Ground Perimeter

The perimeter on the ground and on the slant ignoring any concavities. This measurement is not very useful in gauging the size of a tree, but was much used in the early history of the giant sequoias. It is still useful in calculating the volume of the lowest part of the tree up to the highest point of ground.

Perimeter at High Point of Ground

This perimeter is taken on the level at the highest point of ground.

Perimeter at Breast Height

This perimeter as taken on the level at a height of 4.5 feet above the highest point of ground. This is the standard used by Sequoia and Kings Canyon National Parks. The American Forestry Association uses a level perimeter 4.5 feet above the mean base level. Some coastal redwood measurers use a height of about 5 feet above the mean base.

Volume

Volume is the measurement of the mass of an object. Volume, and not height, is the factor that determines a tree's size. The volume is the number of cubic feet or cubic meters in the main trunk of the tree. This includes the bark, but not the roots, limbs, and foliage.

The volume expressed in cubic feet and cubic meters in this book generally refers to a value calculated by ignoring losses due to burns. Restored volume is given in some sources. Another term is, volume as is, which is the volume ignoring burns minus the volume of the burns. The volume is calculated using trunk diameters and height. I use this formula to calculate volume:

$$V = \frac{(H_1 - H_2)}{12} (D_1^2 + D_1 D_2 + D_2^2)$$

V = volume, H_1 = height at bottom of log, H_2 = height at top of log, D_1 = diameter of bottom of the log and D_2 = diameter at top of log. The diameters are the geometric mean diameter at the given height. The first log is from mean base (0) to high point of ground. The second is from high point of ground to breast height. The third is from breast height to 16 feet, the fourth is from 16 to 30 feet and so on up the tree. Other methods have been used. Ron Hildebrant uses Simpson's rule. Dr. Van Pelt uses a spline curve. Both of these methods give slightly larger volumes than I obtain.

Other Terms

Buttress

The word is used in three different contexts. Used alone the word refers to a protuberance at the base of a tree. A flying buttress occurs when fire has tunneled the tree near its periphery, but not through the center. Examples of this occur in the Stagg Tree, and to an extreme in the Ishi Giant. A limb buttress or flange is a thickened area below a limb that supports the limb. This can lead to exaggerated measurements of the diameter of the tree below the limb. The President Tree in Giant Forest has a number of these, making the true size of the tree difficult to ascertain.

Grove

Man likes to place things in neat little categories, but nature is not very obliging. However, I am going to make a stab at defining what I mean by a grove of giant sequoias.

A grove is (in this book) a giant sequoia population whose seedlings are offspring of the older population. A lobe of a grove is a population that is connected to another part of the grove with a narrow string of sequoias. A unit of a grove is a population that is near the rest of the grove but is narrowly separated from it. To qualify as a unit rather than a separate grove, there should be trees from the units on the same side of a common watershed.

The Forest Service has added an administrative term that refers to a collection of groves or units, all of which are near each other. This is called a complex. Rundel has also used this term to refer to several groups of closely related groves or units.

Large (as applied to giant sequoias and coast redwoods)

A common definition as used in tree inventories taken in the Sequoia and Kings Canyon National Parks refers to a tree that is at least 10.5 feet in diameter at a point 4.5 feet above the high point of ground. Since this is a standard not generally recognized by the compilers of other data gatherers, I have adopted a more relaxed standard of a tree having a diameter of at least 10 feet at breast height. This means that figures given in this book for the number of large trees in a grove or unit is not assumed to be perfectly accurate.

Stem

The main trunk and leader of the tree. Rarely does a giant sequoia have more than one stem. Coastal redwoods commonly have several co-dominate leaders or stems, which complicate comparisons with giant sequoias for trunk volume.

Appendix II: Sequoia and Redwood Superlatives

Largest

Giant sequoia: General Sherman - Giant Forest - 52,508 cubic feet

Coast redwood: Del Norte Titan - Jedediah Smith Redwoods State Park - 37,500 cubic feet

Tallest

Giant sequoia: Unnamed tree - Redwood Mountain Grove - 311 feet

Coast redwood: Stratosphere Giant - Humboldt Redwoods State Park - 369 feet

Oldest

Giant sequoia: 3,200 years or more. Examples in Converse Basin, Mountain Home, and Giant Forest

Coast redwood: 2,000 years or more. Hildebrant claims much older trees.

Other trees: The bristlecone pine – 4,700 years or more. The alerce of Chile - 3,600 years or more.

Greatest Ground Perimeter

Unnamed sequoia, Alder Creek Grove – 155 feet. Freakish tree with enormous basal buttress on very steep ground.

Boole Tree (giant sequoia), Converse Basin – 113.0 feet.

Greatest Maximum Base Diameter

General Grant (giant sequoia), Grant Grove – 40.3 feet.

Unnamed sequoia, Alder Creek Grove – 57 feet. Freakish tree with enormous basal buttress on very steep ground.

Greatest Mean Diameter at Breast Height

General Grant (giant sequoia), Grant Grove – 28.9 feet. Includes part of abnormal buttress.

Washington (giant sequoia), Giant Forest – 26.0 feet.

Lost Monarch (coast redwood), Jedediah Smith Redwoods State Park – 24.9 feet.

Burnt Monarch (dead giant sequoia), Big Stump Grove – About 29 feet if restored (Now 27.7 feet).

Largest Limb

Unnamed sequoia or Arm Tree, Atwell Mill, East Fork Grove – 12.6 feet in diameter.

Thickest Bark

Giant sequoia - Up to about 3 feet.

Highest and Lowest Elevation of Sequoia Natural Occurrence

Highest sequoia: 8,600 feet – East Fork Grove, Atwell Mill.

Lowest sequoia: 2,800 feet – Below Garfield-Dillonwood Grove.

Appendix III: Giant Sequoia Groves

Large trees refer to those 10 feet or more in diameter at breast height. Since every jurisdiction has its own criteria for measuring and classifying trees according to size, it is not surprising that published figures often show some variance. Some groves are poorly documented. Some areas include everything within a perimeter to determine area. Others represent actual coverage by sequoias, which would not count voids within a grove. I have tried to use the most representative data. Sequoias are lost each year, and new ones become large, so counts of the large ones are approximate at best. The number of large trees in the national parks, the state parks, and the Nelder Grove are well documented by inventories. The information on groves on Giant Sequoia National Monument land and other areas are fragmentary at best as to the number of large trees in each grove.

The groves are listed according to their occurrence north to south and west to east. Wherever possible, adjacent groves are next to each other in the list.

Groves

NAME	SIZE	LOCATION, OWNERSHIP, AND COMMENTS
Groves North of the Kings River		
Placer County Grove	6 trees on approx. 3 acres	Tahoe National Forest. Northernmost grove.
North Calaveras Grove	Approx. 70 large trees on 60 acres	Calaveras Big Trees State Park. First well-known grove.
South Calaveras Grove	350 large trees on 445 acres	Calaveras Big Trees State Park.
Tuolomne Grove	20 large trees on 16 acres	Yosemite National Park.
Merced Grove	Approx. 24 large trees on 20 acres	Yosemite National Park.
Mariposa Grove	200 large trees on 230 acres	Yosemite National Park. Two main units.
Nelder Grove	100 large trees on 280 to 350 acres	Sierra National Forest, California Institute of Technology and private land. Four scattered units. Heavily logged of sequoias.
Kings River Groves		
McKinley Grove	74 large trees on 80 acres	Sierra National Forest.
Converse Basin	Approx. 70 large trees on 3,535 acres	Giant Sequoia National Monument. Includes Cabin Creek and Boole Tree groves, lobes of main grove. Logged of most sequoias. Several very old cut trees.
Indian Basin Grove	218 acres	Giant Sequoia National Monument. All large sequoias have been logged.
Lockwood Grove	Approx. 25 large trees on 120 acres	Giant Sequoia National Monument. Two units; west unit heavily logged.
Evan's Grove	Approx. 500 large trees on 1,600 acres	Giant Sequoia National Monument. Includes Horseshoe Bend and Windy Gulch "groves". Detached unit to north.
Kennedy Grove	Approx. 200 large trees on 350 acres	Giant Sequoia National Monument. Two narrowly separated units. South unit also called Burton Grove.
Little Boulder Creek Grove	Approx. 100 large trees on 102 acres	Giant Sequoia National Monument.
Boulder Creek Grove	Approx. 30 large trees on 40 acres	Giant Sequoia National Monument.

Note: Unnamed complex. The Agnew, Deer Meadow and Monarch groves are narrowly separated units of a grove complex.

NAME	SIZE	LOCATION, OWNERSHIP, AND COMMENTS
Monarch Grove	Possibly 8 large trees on about 100 acres	Monarch Wilderness. Recently re-discovered grove.
Agnew Grove	Approx. 40 large trees on 112 acres	Giant Sequoia National Monument. Two units called Agnew North and Agnew South groves.
Deer Meadow Grove	Approx. 60 large trees on 278 acres	Giant Sequoia National Monument.

NAME	SIZE	LOCATION, OWNERSHIP, AND COMMENTS
Bearskin Grove	Possibly 20 large trees on 68 acres	Giant Sequoia National Monument.
Landslide Grove	Approx. 50 large trees on 86 acres	Giant Sequoia National Monument. Perhaps 2 units.
Cherry Gap Grove	No large sequoias on 90 acres	Giant Sequoia National Monument. All large sequoias have been logged.
Abbott Creek Grove	No large sequoias on 5 acres	Giant Sequoia National Monument. All large sequoias have been logged.
Grant Grove	190 large trees on 251 acres	Kings Canyon National Park and Giant Sequoia National Monument. Largest tree is General Grant.
Sequoia Creek Grove	15 large trees on 20 acres	Kings Canyon National Park and small part on private land.
Big Stump Grove	Approx. 17 large trees on 398 acres	Kings Canyon National Park and Giant Sequoia National Monument.

Kaweah River Groves

NAME	SIZE	LOCATION, OWNERSHIP, AND COMMENTS
Redwood Mountain Grove	Approx. 2,359 large trees on about 4,500 acres	Kings Canyon National Park, Giant Sequoia National Monument, University of California, and private land. Mostly in Kings Canyon National Park. About 500 acres outside of park. West edge partially logged of sequoias on university and Giant Sequoia National Monument land.
Muir Grove	248 large trees on 235 acres	Sequoia National Park.
Lost Grove	56 large trees on 46 acres	Sequoia National Park.
Pine Ridge Grove	18 large trees on 39 acres	Sequoia National Park. Two units. New acreage recently reported.
Skagway Grove	61 large trees on 66 acres	Sequoia National Park. Two units.
Suwanee Grove	56 large trees on 67 acres	Sequoia National Park.
Giant Forest	2,261 large trees on 2,112 acres	Sequoia National Park. Includes General Sherman Tree.
Castle Creek Grove (a complex)	98 large trees on 197 acres	Sequoia National Park. Three or four close units. Area may be larger than reported here.
Redwood Meadow (a complex)	202 large trees on 261 acres	Sequoia National Park. Four somewhat separated units called Redwood Meadow, Little Redwood Meadow, Granite Creek, Cliff Creek.

NAME	SIZE	LOCATION, OWNERSHIP, AND COMMENTS
Case Mountain (a complex)	40 large trees on 55 acres	Bureau of Land Management and private land. Now consists of four scattered units. Other areas almost completely logged of sequoias. Original area probably much larger.
Coffeepot Canyon Grove	5 large trees on 9 acres	Sequoia National Park.
Eden Creek Grove	273 large trees on 366 acres	Sequoia National Park. At least three units.
Cahoon Creek Grove	13 large trees on 12 acres	Sequoia National Park. Very close to Horse Creek Grove.
Horse Creek Grove	25 large trees on 43 acres	Sequoia National Park.
Squirrel Creek Grove	One large tree on 2 acres	Sequoia National Park. Could be considered remote unit of Oriole Grove. Mostly logged of sequoias.
Oriole Grove	147 trees on 132 acres	Sequoia National Park. Separate unit to north.
New Oriole Grove	11 large trees on 21 acres	Sequoia National Park.
Atwell-East Grove complex	1,270 trees on 2,191 acres	Mostly in Sequoia National Park. Part on private land. This is a complex of groves. Tenuous connecting links between Atwell lobe and main East Fork lobe. There are two other units, Redwood Creek Grove and a unit well upstream from the main East Fork lobe. Atwell lobe has 880 large trees on 1,335 acres. One corner logged of sequoias. East Fork lobe has 350 large trees of 751 acres. Redwood Creek unit has 36 large trees on 223 acres. A few large trees in the small east unit of the East Fork lobe.
Surprise Grove	One large tree on 4 acres	Sequoia National Park. Additional area reported recently.
Homer's Nose Grove	108 large trees on 245 acres	Sequoia National Park. Includes Cedar Flat Grove, a downstream lobe.
Board Camp Grove	31 large trees on 55 acres	Sequoia National Park.
South Fork Grove	131 large trees on 210 acres	Sequoia National Park.
Devil's Canyon Grove	10 large trees on 6 acres	Sequoia National Park. Two remote outliers lie far to the north. Grove may be bigger than stated here.
Garfield-Dillonwood Grove	1,500 large trees on 3,088 acres	Sequoia National Park and Giant Sequoia National Monument.

NAME	SIZE	LOCATION, OWNERSHIP, AND COMMENTS
Tule River and other Southern Groves		
Dennison Grove	9 large trees on 11 acres	Sequoia National Park.
Dillonwood	See Garfield-Dillonwood Grove	Dillonwood refers to the southern lobe of the Garfield-Dillonwood Grove. Previously on private land, Dillonwood recently became part of Sequoia National Park.
Mountain Home Groves Complex	1,200 large trees on 3,200 acres. Data uncertain.	Mountain Home State Forest, Giant Sequoia National Monument, and Tulare County (Balch Park). A large complex of groves with three main lobes and several isolated units to the west of the main body of trees, and a unit above and west of Middle Tule lobe called Moses Mountain Grove. Silver Creek Grove appears to be very tenuously connected to the main lobe of the grove to the east. It has a small unit south of Silver Creek on Forest Service land. Significant areas logged of sequoias.
Maggie Mountain	Approx. 50 large trees on 66 acres	Giant Sequoia National Monument. Two units named Maggie Mountain North and South.
Burro Creek Grove	Approx. 100 large trees on 302 acres	Giant Sequoia National Monument. Two acres on Mountain Home State Forest.
Wishon Grove	Approx. 30 large trees on 171 acres	Giant Sequoia National Monument. Recently identified grove (1994). May be the incorrectly mapped North Alder Creek Grove.
Alder Creek Grove	Approx. 200 large trees on 733 acres	Private land and Giant Sequoia National Monument. Private land covers 495 acres.
McIntyre Grove The Forest Service administration name is Belknap Complex.	Approx. 900 large trees on 2,049 acres	Mostly on Giant Sequoia National Monument with 90 acres on private land. This is a complex consisting of four major areas that are actually contiguous: Wheel Meadow, McIntyre, Belknap Camp groves, and an unnamed lobe. There are several outlying groups.
Black Mountain Complex (Black Mountain Grove)	Approx. 1,000 trees on 3,130 acres	Giant Sequoia National Monument, Tule River Indian Reservation and private land. Consists of a large section on the north side of Solo Peak, and a somewhat fragmented area on the south side of Solo Peak consisting of at least four units, three to the west and one to the east of the main grove. This grove is misnamed, as Black Mountain is to the west of the grove. Parts of the grove have been logged of sequoias.
Red Hill Grove	Possibly 50 large trees on 631 acres	Giant Sequoia National Monument, private land and Tule River Indian Reservation.

NAME	SIZE	LOCATION, OWNERSHIP, AND COMMENTS
Peyrone Grove	Possibly 100 large trees on 520 acres	Giant Sequoia National Monument and Tule River Indian Reservation.
South Peyrone Grove	Possibly 20 large trees on 33 acres	Giant Sequoia National Monument and possibly on Tule River Indian Reservation.
North Cold Spring Grove	Possibly 10 large trees on 17 acres	Tule River Indian Reservation.
Parker Peak Grove	100 large trees on 300 acres	Tule River Indian Reservation.

Kern River Groves

Freeman Creek Grove	Approx. 700 large trees on 1800 acres	Giant Sequoia National Monument and private land.
Long Meadow Grove	Approx. 100 large trees on about 250 acres	Giant Sequoia National Monument.
Cunningham Grove	Approx. 5 large trees on 10 acres	Giant Sequoia National Monument.
Packsaddle Grove	Approx. 100 large trees on 317 acres	Giant Sequoia National Monument.
Starvation Creek Complex	Approx. 30 large trees on 21 acres	Giant Sequoia National Monument.
Deer Creek Grove	30 large trees on 40 acres	Giant Sequoia National Monument.

Note: Some sources list two units of one grove as two groves.

Appendix IV: Giant Sequoia and Coast Redwood Data

Table I -
Ranking of giant sequoias whose volume exceeds 30,000 cubic feet
Measurements are shown in feet and volume in cubic feet. The names in parenthesis are unofficial designations proposed by the author.

TREE	GROVE AND LOCATION	VOLUME	HEIGHT	GROUND PERIMETER	MEAN BASE DIAMETER	DIAMETER AT BREAST HEIGHT
1 General Sherman	Giant Forest, SNP	52,508	274.9	102.6	30.3	25.1
2 Washington	Giant Forest, SNP	47,850	254.7	101.1	30.9	26.0
3 General Grant	Grant Grove, KCNP	46,608	268.1	107.5	31.8	28.9
4 President	Giant Forest, SNP	45,148	240.9	93.0	28.3	23.1
5 Lincoln	Giant Forest, SNP	44,471	255.8	98.3	30.0	24.5
6 Amos Alonzo Stagg	Alder Creek, Private	42,557	243.0	109.0	29.0	22.8
7 Boole	Converse Basin, GSNM	42,472	268.8	113.0	32.2	25.4
8 Genesis	Mountain Home, MHSF	41,897	253.0	85.3	25.9	22.5
9 (Franklin)	Giant Forest, SNP	41,280	223.8	94.8	28.4	21.9
10 (King Arthur)	Garfield, SNP	40,656	270.3	104.2	28.7	23.1
11 (Monroe)	Giant Forest, SNP	40,104	247.8	91.3	27.9	23.4
12 Robert E. Lee	Grant Grove, KCNP	40,102	254.7	88.3	26.8	23.8
13 (Adams)	Giant Forest, SNP	38,956	250.6	83.3	25.7	20.5
14 Ishi Giant	Kennedy, GSNM	38,156	255.0	105.1	31.5	25.5
15 (Column or Near Pershing)	Giant Forest, SNP	37,295	243.8	93.0	27.6	23.3
16 (Summit Road)	Mt. Home, MHSF	36,600	244.0	82.2	24.5	20.6
17 (Euclid)	Mt. Home, MHSF	36,122	272.7	83.4	24.4	20.3
18 Washington	Mariposa, YNP	35,901	236.0	95.7	28.5	23.8
19 Pershing	Giant Forest, SNP	35,855	246.0	91.2	26.3	21.5
20 (Diamond)	Atwell Mill, SNP	35,292	286.0	95.3	26.9	18.4

TREE	GROVE AND LOCATION	VOLUME	HEIGHT	GROUND PERIMETER	MEAN BASE DIAMETER	DIAMETER AT BREAST HEIGHT
21 Adam	Mt. Home, MHSF	35,017	247.4	94.2	28.6	23.0
22 (Roosevelt or False Hart)	Redwood Mt., KCNP	35,013	260.0	80.0	24.2	22.2
23 Nelder	Nelder, Sierra Nat. Forest	34,993	266.2	90.0	25.8	21.0
24 (AD)	Atwell Mill, SNP	34,706	242.4	99.0	24.1	17.8
25 Hart	Redwood Mt., KCNP	34,407	277.9	75.3	23.5	21.3
26 Grizzly Giant	Mariposa, YNP	34,005	209.0	92.5	29.5	25.4
27 Chief Sequoyah	Giant Forest, SNP	33,608	228.2	90.4	27.4	20.7
28 Methuselah	Mt. Home, MHSF	32,897	207.8	95.8	29.7	24.0
29 Great Goshawk	Freeman Creek, GSNM	32,783	255.2	90.2	28.5	23.1
30 (Hamilton)	Giant Forest, SNP	32,783	238.5	82.6	26.0	22.0
31 Dean	Atwell Mill, SNP	32,333	235.8	96.3	27.0	20.3
32 (Black Mt. Beauty)	Black Mt., GSNM	32,224	262.7	75.8	22.5	19.1
33 Packsaddle Giant	Packsaddle, GSNM	32,156	218.0	106.3	32.4	24.3
34 Allen Russell	Mt. Home, MHSF	31,606	253.9	79.7	25.0	21.7
35 Cleveland	Giant Forest, SNP	31,336	250.5	79.8	24.7	22.9
36 Agassiz	South Calaveras, CSP	30,580	262.0	97.0	29.0	22.3
37 (Near Ed by Ned)	Giant Forest, SNP	30,333	250.8	79.4	24.2	19.8
38 Evans Tree	Evans, GSNM	30,232	232.4	77.5	22.7	17.7
39 (Three Fingered Jack)	Mt. Home, MHSF	30,118	239.9	82.5	23.0	18.6
40 Patriarch	McIntyre, GSNM	30,020	176.4	72.6	22.6	19.3

Names in parenthesis are unofficial names

Key:

KCNP = KINGS CANYON NATIONAL PARK

YNP = YOSEMITE NATIONAL PARK

SNP = SEQUOIA NATIONAL PARK

MHSF = MOUNTAIN HOME STATE PARK

GSNM = GIANT SEQUOIA NATIONAL MONUMENT (IN SEQUOIA NATIONAL FOREST)

CSP = CALAVERAS BIG TREES STATE PARK

Table II - Coast redwoods whose volume exceeds 30,000 cubic feet.

Abbreviations

JSRSP = JEDEDIAH SMITH REDWOODS STATE PARK
PCRSP = PRAIRIE CREEK REDWOODS STATE PARK
HRSP = HUMBOLDT REDWOODS STATE PARK
RNP = REDWOOD NATIONAL PARK

TREE	LOCATION	VOLUME	DIAMETER BREAST HIGH	HEIGHT
1. Del Norte Titan	JSRSP	36,893 cubic feet	23.7 feet	307 feet
2. Iluvatar	PCRSP	36,473	20.5	300
3. Lost Monarch	JSRSP	34,914	26.0	320
4. Howland Hill Giant	JSRSP	33,581	19.1	330
5. Sir Isaac Newton	PCRSP	33,192	22.5	299
6. El Viejo Del Norte	JSRSP	32,644	23.0	330
7. Terex Giant	PCRSP	32,384	23.0	270
8. Adventure Tree	PCRSP	32,140	16.5	341
9. Bull Creek Giant	HRSP	31,144	21.0	337
10. Arco Giant	RNP	30,699	22.5	262

Michael Taylor of the *Tall Trees Club* provided the data in the table of the largest known Coast redwoods. Data represents the collective efforts of Michael Taylor, Steve Sillett, Ron Hildebrant, Robert Van Pelt, and Chris Atkins.

Appendix V: References

Cook, Lawrence F. *The Giant Sequoias of California*. Washington D.C.: U. S. Department of the Interior, National Park Service, 1942.

EngBeck, Joseph H. Jr. *The Enduring Giants*. Berkeley, CA: University of California, 1973.

Fry, Walter and White, John R. *Big Trees*. Stanford University, CA: Stanford University Press, Eighth printing 1945.

Hartesveldt, Richard J., et al. *The Giant Sequoia of the Sierra Nevada*. Washington D. C.: U. S. Department of the Interior, 1975.

Harvey, H. Thomas, et al. *Giant Sequoia Ecology*. Washington D. C.: U.S. Department of the Interior, National Park Service, 1980.

Harvey, H. Thomas. *The Sequoias of Yosemite National Park*. Yosemite National Park, CA: Yosemite Natural History Association, 1978.

Johnson, Hank. *They Felled the Redwoods*. Fish Camp, CA: Trans-Amglo Books, 1976.

Muir, John. *Sierra Big Trees*. Golden, Co: Outbooks, 1980.

Otter, Floyd L. *The Men of Mammoth Forest*. Floyd Leslie Otter, 1982.

Rogers, Bob. Giant sequoia specialist who worked for Sequoia National Forest. Personal correspondence and private conversations.

Rundel, Philip W. *An Annotated Check List of the Groves of Sequoiadendron giganteum in the Sierra Nevada, California*. Reprinted from Madroño, Volume 21, Number 5, Part One, January 1972.

White, John R. and Pusateri, Samuel J. *Sequoia and Kings Canyon National Parks*. Stanford University, CA: Stanford University Press, 1949.

Willard, Dwight. *Giant Sequoia Groves of the Sierra Nevada*. 2nd ed. Berkeley, CA: Dwight Willard, 1995.

Willard, Dwight. Personal correspondence.

Appendix VI: Suggested Reading

Fry, Walter and White, John R. *Big Trees*. 8th ed. Stanford University, CA: Stanford University Press. 1945.

Hartesveldt, Richard J., et al. *The Giant Sequoia of the Sierra Nevada*. Washington D. C.: U. S. Department of the Interior, 1975.

Harvey, H. Thomas. *The Sequoias of Yosemite National Park*. Yosemite National Park, CA: Yosemite Natural History Association, 1978.

Johnston, Hank. *They Felled the Redwoods*. Fish Camp, CA: Stauffer Publishing, 1996.

Johnston, Verna R. *California Forests and Woodlands*. Berkeley, CA: University of California Press, 1994.

Hartesveldt. R.J. et al. *Giant Sequoias*. Three Rivers, CA: Sequoia Natural History Association, 1981.

Kelley, Margaret S. *Congress Trail Sequoia National Park*. Three Rivers, CA: Sequoia Natural History Association, 1978.

Muir, John. *Sierra Big Trees*. Golden, CO: Outbooks, 1980.

Tweed, William. *The General Sherman Tree*. Three Rivers, CA: Sequoia Natural History Association, 1988.

Tweed, William and Lary Dilsaver. *Challenge of the Big Trees*. Three Rivers, CA: Sequoia Natural History Association, 1990.

Tweed, William. *Beneath the Giants: A Guide to the Moro Rock Crescent Meadow Road of Sequoia National Park*. Three Rivers, CA: Sequoia Natural History Association, 1985.

Van Pelt, Robert. *Forest Giants of the Pacific Coast*. Vancouver, Canada and San Francisco: Global Forest Society, 2001.

Willard, Dwight. *A Guide to the Giant Sequoia Groves of California*. Yosemite National Park, CA: Yosemite Association, 2000.

Books for Children:

Bosveld, Jane. *While a Tree was Growing*. New York: American Museum of Natural History, 1977.

Ohanian, Susan. *California's Giant Sequoias*. Worthington, OH: SRA/McGraw-Hill, 1996.

Schneider, Bill. *The Giant Trees, the Story of the Redwoods, the World's Largest Trees*. Billings, MT: Falcon Press Publishing Company, 1988.

Wadsworth, Ginger. *Giant Sequoia Trees*. Minneapolis, MN: Lerner Publications Company, 1995.

Appendix VII: Notes

Chapter 1

1. Fry, Walter and White, John R. *Big Trees*. Stanford University Press, 1939, p. 8.

2. Fry and White, p. 8.

3. Fry and White, p. 8.

4. Hartesveldt, Richard J., et al. *The Giant Sequoia of the Sierra Nevada*. Washington D.C.: U.S. Department of the Interior, 1975.

5. Fry and White, p. 9.

6. Fry and White, p. 9.

7. Hartesveldt.

8. Fry and White, p. 11.

9. The Jourdan Report. 1931. Fresno Junior Chamber of Commerce.

10. The Jourdan Report.

11. Sequoia National Park, National Park Service files.

12. Fern Gray. *And The Giants Were Named*, Sequoia Natural History Association.

13. Data derived from Dr. Robert Van Pelt.

Chapter 2

1. Willard, Dwight. *Giant Sequoia Groves of the Sierra Nevada*. 2nd ed. Berkeley, CA: Dwight Willard, 1995.

2. Fry and White, pp. 8-9.

3. Dr. Robert Van Pelt, personal correspondence.

4. Evans, Oscar M. Early. Forest Examiner. U.S. Department of Agriculture, Forest Service map of North Calaveras Grove.

5. Evans Cruise list and *A Guide to the Calaveras North Grove Trail*. Calaveras Big Trees State Park, CA: Calaveras Big Trees Association, 1990.

6. Most data from Evans Cruise list and *A Guide to the Calaveras North Grove Trail*. Calaveras Big Trees State Park, CA: Calaveras Big Trees Association, 1990.

7. Dion, Carl. Mapping and Cruising the Tuolumne Grove. Yosemite National Park Library, 1906. Unpublished paper.

8. Bellue, Alfred J. 1930 unpublished report, Yosemite National Park.

9. Willard, Dwight. *Giant Sequoia Groves of the Sierra Nevada*. 2nd ed. Berkeley, CA: Dwight Willard, 1995.

10. Hutchinson, Stan. Personal correspondence.

11. Kruska, Dennis G. *Sierra Nevada Big Trees, History of Exhibitions, 1850 – 1903*. Los Angeles: Dawson's Bookshop, 1985.

Chapter 3

1. Gray.

2. Gray.

3. Gray. There are conflicting reports as to the legality of the cutting of this tree and the consequences, if any, sustained by the offenders.

4. Jourdan report.

5. Hartesveldt.

6. Dr. Donald J. McGraw. Personal communication.

7. Bob Rogers. Personal communication.

8. From the *Expositor*, city unknown, possibly Visalia, published in 1908.

Chapter 4

1. Fern Gray.

2. Personal letter from Pat Hart.

3. Gray.

4. Gray.

5. Gray.

6. Gray.

7. *Daily Alta Californian*, San Francisco, CA, August 20, 1888.

Chapter 5

1. Otter, Floyd L. *The Men of Mammoth Forest*. 4th ed. Floyd Leslie Otter, 1982.

2. Otter.

3. Otter.

4. Otter.

5. Otter.

Chapter 6

1. Evans, Oscar M. Early, 1936 timber survey.

2. Douglas Leisz, personal communication.

3. Forest Clingan, personal communication.

4. *Field and Stream*, Dec. 1935, full citation.

5. Guy Hughs, *Bakersfield Californian*, 1961.

6. Frank Cunningham, personal communication.

7. *Daily Alta Californian*, 1879.

8. Frank Cunningham, personal communication.

Chapter 7

1. Dr. Robert Van Pelt (personal communications). Additional information from Ron Hildebrant, Michael Taylor, Rudolf W. Becking, and Frank Clark.

Index